INTRODUCING
ISSUES WITH
OPPOSING
VIEWPOINTS®

Debt

Christina Fisanick, *Book Editor*

GREENHAVEN PRESS
A part of Gale, Cengage Learning

GALE
CENGAGE Learning·

Detroit • New York • San Francisco • New Haven, Conn • Waterville, Maine • London

Elizabeth Des Chenes, *Director, Publishing Solutions*

For more information, contact:
Greenhaven Press
27500 Drake Rd.
Farmington Hills, MI 48331-3535
Or you can visit our Internet site at gale.cengage.com

For product information and technology assistance, contact us at

Gale Customer Support, 1-800-877-4253
For permission to use material from this text or product, submit all requests online at
www.cengage.com/permissions

Further permissions questions can be e-mailed to permissionrequest@cengage.com

Articles in Greenhaven Press anthologies are often edited for length to meet page requirements. In addition, original titles of these works are changed to clearly present the main thesis and to explicitly indicate the author's opinion. Every effort is made to ensure that Greenhaven Press accurately reflects the original intent of the authors. Every effort has been made to trace the owners of copyrighted material.

Cover image © Dmitriy Shironosov/Shutterstock.com.

LIBRARY OF CONGRESS CATALOGING-IN-PUBLICATION DATA
Debt / Christina Fisanick, book editor.
pages cm. -- (Introducing issues with opposing viewpoints)
Includes bibliographical references and index.
ISBN 978-0-7377-5673-9 (hardcover)
1. Consumer credit--Juvenile literature. 2. Debt--Juvenile literature. I. Fisanick, Christina.
HG3755.D43 2013
332.7'43--dc23
2012044606

Printed in the United States of America
1 2 3 4 5 6 7 17 16 15 14 13

Contents

Indulging in a wide spectrum of ideas, beliefs, and perspectives is a critical cornerstone of democracy. After all, it is often debates over differences of opinion, such as whether to legalize abortion, how to treat prisoners, or when to enact the death penalty, that shape our society and drive it forward. Such diversity of thought is frequently regarded as the hallmark of a healthy and civilized culture. As the Reverend Clifford Schutjer of the First Congregational Church in Mansfield, Ohio, declared in a 2001 sermon, "Surrounding oneself with only like-minded people, restricting what we listen to or read only to what we find agreeable is irresponsible. Refusing to entertain doubts once we make up our minds is a subtle but deadly form of arrogance." With this advice in mind, Introducing Issues with Opposing Viewpoints books aim to open readers' minds to the critically divergent views that comprise our world's most important debates.

Introducing Issues with Opposing Viewpoints simplifies for students the enormous and often overwhelming mass of material now available via print and electronic media. Collected in every volume is an array of opinions that captures the essence of a particular controversy or topic. Introducing Issues with Opposing Viewpoints books embody the spirit of nineteenth-century journalist Charles A. Dana's axiom: "Fight for your opinions, but do not believe that they contain the whole truth, or the only truth." Absorbing such contrasting opinions teaches students to analyze the strength of an argument and compare it to its opposition. From this process readers can inform and strengthen their own opinions, or be exposed to new information that will change their minds. Introducing Issues with Opposing Viewpoints is a mosaic of different voices. The authors are statesmen, pundits, academics, journalists, corporations, and ordinary people who have felt compelled to share their experiences and ideas in a public forum. Their words have been collected from newspapers, journals, books, speeches, interviews, and the Internet, the fastest growing body of opinionated material in the world.

Introducing Issues with Opposing Viewpoints shares many of the well-known features of its critically acclaimed parent series, Opposing Viewpoints. The articles are presented in a pro/con format, allowing readers to absorb divergent perspectives side by side. Active reading questions preface each viewpoint, requiring the student to approach the material thoughtfully and carefully. Useful charts, graphs, and cartoons supplement each article. A thorough introduction provides readers with crucial background on an issue. An annotated bibliography points the reader toward articles, books, and websites that contain additional information on the topic. An appendix of organizations to contact contains a wide variety of charities, nonprofit organizations, political groups, and private enterprises that each hold a position on the issue at hand. Finally, a comprehensive index allows readers to locate content quickly and efficiently.

Introducing Issues with Opposing Viewpoints is also significantly different from Opposing Viewpoints. As the series title implies, its presentation will help introduce students to the concept of opposing viewpoints and learn to use this material to aid in critical writing and debate. The series' four-color, accessible format makes the books attractive and inviting to readers of all levels. In addition, each viewpoint has been carefully edited to maximize a reader's understanding of the content. Short but thorough viewpoints capture the essence of an argument. A substantial, thought-provoking essay question placed at the end of each viewpoint asks the student to further investigate the issues raised in the viewpoint, compare and contrast two authors' arguments, or consider how one might go about forming an opinion on the topic at hand. Each viewpoint contains sidebars that include at-a-glance information and handy statistics. A Facts About section located in the back of the book further supplies students with relevant facts and figures.

Following in the tradition of the Opposing Viewpoints series, Greenhaven Press continues to provide readers with invaluable exposure to the controversial issues that shape our world. As John Stuart Mill once wrote: "The only way in which a human being can make some approach to knowing the whole of a subject is by hearing what can be said about it by persons of every variety of opinion and studying all modes in which it can be looked at by every character of mind. No wise man ever acquired his wisdom in any mode but this." It is to this principle that Introducing Issues with Opposing Viewpoints books are dedicated.

Introduction

"America is on the verge of becoming a country in decline—economically stagnant and permanently debt-bound, less prosperous, and less free. But this fate does not have to be our future."

— J.D. Foster, "Beyond the Debt Limit, Saving the American Dream"

In her introduction to *How Debt Bankrupts the Middle Class*, editor Katherine Porter attributes the 1.5 million bankruptcies filed by American families in 2010 to an increase in consumption paid for by debt. She argues that the spending boom that fueled the economy in the late twentieth century is now responsible for a decline in the middle class, and "by all indicators, consumer debt will be a defining feature of middle-class families for years to come." Few experts would argue against Porter's reasoning, given that the average household owes in excess of $20,000, bringing the total debt owed by all Americans to a staggering $11.38 trillion, according to the Federal Reserve. However, experts continue to debate the causes of the current debt crisis, which in turn has prevented the finding of a solution.

Many Americans rely on credit to pay for everything from cars to homes to even everyday necessities, but this way of thinking is a recent trend. Credit did not become readily available to most people until the 1970s. Even then, the use of credit was restricted to wealthier citizens. In around the mid-1980s, when laws were passed to limit regulations on financial institutions and the interest rates they charged, more people began to use credit. Before long, many Americans were living beyond their means, largely because incomes and personal wealth rose much more slowly than did the amount of money borrowed.

Some economists argue that this unbalanced situation was the result of companies exporting, or outsourcing, their jobs overseas. In the March 3, 2010, issue of the *Huffington Post*, Mike Elk writes, "Since 2000, the U.S. has lost 5.5 million manufacturing jobs, with 2.1 million of those jobs being lost in the last two years alone. Since 2001, over 42,400 factories have closed in the U.S., and another

90,000 are considered at severe risk of closing." Rather than curtail spending or risk homelessness, those Americans who found themselves underemployed or unemployed by losing their jobs to outsourcing fell further and further into debt.

Nonetheless, corporations that moved jobs overseas during this period say that they were forced to do so because they could no longer afford the high wages demanded by American workers or because of too-strict government regulations. In addition, some company executives, including the late Apple CEO and founder Steve Jobs, insist that there are not enough highly skilled workers in the United States to do the jobs that they need done. In the June 20, 2011, edition of the *Financial Times*, Eric Siegel, chief executive in the United States for Siemens, the German manufacturing company, noted, "There's a mismatch between the jobs that are available, at least in our portfolio, and the people that we see out there. There is a shortage [of workers with the right skills]."

Proponents of higher education agree that having an educated, well-trained populace is essential for the health and wealth of the nation. According to the Center for Education Statistics, "In 2010, the median of earnings for young adults with a bachelor's degree was $45,000, while the median was $21,000 for those without a high school diploma or its equivalent, $29,900 for those with a high school diploma or its equivalent, and $37,000 for those with an associate's degree." Obviously, obtaining a college degree can make a substantial difference in earning potential and lifestyle options. More income means more spending and, perhaps, less debt.

On the other hand, college is expensive and becoming increasingly more so as tuitions rise and student aid diminishes. The Canadian-based investment firm Brockhouse and Cooper estimate that since 2001, college tuitions have increased by 57 percent, while the average rate of pay made by college graduates fell by 7 percent during the same period. Some financial experts are recommending for the first time in decades that college be delayed or avoided altogether by people who cannot afford it because it only leads to debt that cannot easily be repaid. According to FinAid's Student Loan Debt Clock, student loan debt is increasing by $2,853.88 per second. In 2012 it surpassed $1 trillion. Clearly, the cost of college weighs heavily on the backs of all Americans, but especially those families in search of the American dream.

In the midst of increasing unemployment and the climbing costs of higher education, Americans are still digging out of the housing bust, which resulted in the loss of millions of homes nationwide. The housing market reached its peak in 2006 in terms of housing costs and loans granted. Never before were consumers with poor credit ratings given the opportunity to own homes, but the market could not hold. By 2007 it was clear that many homeowners were in over the heads with their mortgages. In an effort to save homeowners and the companies that financed their mortgages, the federal government bailed out Freddie Mac (Federal Home Loan Mortgage Corporation, or FHLMC) and Fannie Mae (Federal National Mortgage Association, or FNMA) in 2009. The good news is that most economists say that the housing crisis has passed. In the July 11, 2012, issue of the *Wall Street Journal*, David Wessel predicts, "From here on, housing is unlikely to drag the U.S. economy down further."

Obviously, these factors and many others have impacted consumer confidence and the way of life of many Americans, especially the middle class, which has been a strong force in the economy for decades. The authors in *Introducing Issues with Opposing Viewpoints: Debt* argue that many people are responsible for educating themselves and others about the benefits and disadvantages of debt and the long-term consequences of lending and borrowing on the personal and national level. What the future holds remains unclear, but it is certain that America has a long way to go to be a debt-free nation.

Chapter 1

How Should Teens Manage Debt?

Managing debt can be difficult for teenagers.

The Government Should Help Young People Avoid Debt

> *"It's time to adopt something similar [to graduated driver's licenses] to ease teenagers into their financial responsibilities."*

Liz Pulliam Weston

Liz Pulliam Weston is a widely read contributor to MSN Money and the author of the nationally syndicated column *Money Talk*. In the following viewpoint she argues that the government should issue restrictions to protect young people from ruining their credit. She states that teenagers should be given a debt driver's license, which involves graduated restrictions in three main areas of debt: credit cards, student loans, and car loans. She asserts that by giving young people credit privileges that grow over time, they can learn responsible money management skills. In addition, she argues that the government should pass laws to protect teens from predatory lenders who take advantage of their financial ignorance.

G raduated drivers' licenses—which restrict when and with whom young people can drive—seem to do a pretty good job reducing auto accidents and fatalities.

Perhaps it's time to adopt something similar to ease teenagers into their financial responsibilities.

Right now, adolescents can sign themselves up for life-crushing debt years before they can legally drink, and sometimes before they're even old enough to vote. Some of this debt—specifically, student loans— can literally follow them to the grave, since it typically can't be erased in bankruptcy court.

We've talked ourselves blue in the face about the need for financial literacy education, and it isn't working. The little that is getting taught is being overwhelmed by the relentless marketing of student loan companies, credit card issuers and other lenders.

Senator Dodd's Proposal

I'm not the only one who thinks we need to do something drastic to prevent another generation from being enslaved by debt. Recently, Sen. Christopher Dodd, D-Conn., introduced a bill that would place unprecedented restrictions on credit card issuers that target teenagers.

The Credit Card Accountability Responsibility and Disclosure Act of 2009 would forbid card issuers from opening accounts for people under 21 unless one of these criteria is met:

- A parent, guardian or other responsible individual agrees to co-sign for the debt.
- The applicant provides proof he or she can independently repay the debt.

- Proof is provided that the applicant has completed a certified financial literacy course.

The bill also would prohibit credit bureaus from adding people under 21 to the marketing lists they sell lenders and others without the young people's consent. People under 21 would have to "opt in," or give their permission, to receive credit card solicitations.

The bill is good as far as it goes, which is about a country mile short of far enough.

The Author's Proposal

Here's what I propose.

No credit cards until you're 21. Instead, you can have a charge card, which will help you learn to use credit the right way: as a convenience, rather than a tool to live beyond your means.

President Barack Obama signs the Credit Card Accountability Responsibility and Disclosure Act of 2009. The law forbids card issuers from opening accounts for people under age twenty-one unless specific criteria are met.

Credit cards allow you to carry, or "revolve" in industry terms, a balance. Young people with tiny credit histories get charged usurious interest rates for the privilege of failing to pay off their balances.

By contrast, a charge card requires you to pay your balance in full every month. Used properly, it can help build your credit history. (The most famous charge cards are the traditional green and gold cards offered by American Express.)

This is somewhat analogous to graduated licensing requirements that require young drivers to go solo or travel only with a responsible adult. This restriction helps novice drivers learn good habits by limiting distractions.

One of the Smartest Things to Do

And that is what minimum payments, teaser interest rates and the other trappings of credit cards are: distractions from the key habit of paying your balance in full every month. Inculcating this habit is one of the smartest things we can do for the next generation. If they can learn that, their odds of getting rich soar, and their odds of filing bankruptcy plummet.

Charge cards to people under 21 should be issued according to Sen. Dodd's restrictions: Applicants would need parental OK, proof of independent income or completion of a financial literacy course.

Will bankers issue charge cards if their young customers can't be sheared with outrageous interest rates? Some won't, but others are sure to see the opportunity in earning young customers' loyalty early on.

No Payday Loans

The military finally chased these bloodsuckers away from their bases by prohibiting anyone from charging a soldier interest rates in excess of 36%. Since the annual percentage rate of a typical payday loan is around 400%, this was an effective strategy.

But there are still more payday lending outlets in the U.S. than McDonald's and Burger King restaurants—*combined.* Payday lenders prey on the financially unsophisticated, who don't understand that a short-term cash advance loan can easily spiral into unmanageable debt.

Perhaps Congress one day will put legal loan sharks out of business, but in the meantime we can demand that payday lenders stop preying on our kids. In fact, I'd restrict anyone under 21 from even entering a payday lenders' premises, so young children wouldn't have to be witnesses as their parents ruin their financial lives.

This would be the curfew component of the financial driver's license. Graduated licenses typically demand young drivers stay off the road at night, because that's when the seriously bad stuff happens. Keep kids out of payday lenders, and the chances of seriously bad stuff is a heck of a lot less.

No Private Student Loans Without a Waiver

To understand why this is important, I'll need to give you a quick tutorial in education funding.

Student loans come in two basic flavors: federal and private. Federal student loans these days are the bee's knees: They have low fixed interest rates and flexible repayment plans. It's virtually impossible to overdose on them before you're 21, since the total amount you can borrow as a typical undergraduate is limited to $31,000. Even those college graduates who wind up in lower-paid professions, such as teaching, should be able to handle the payments.

FAST FACT

According to Janet Bodnar of *Kiplinger's Personal Finance*, 35 percent of teens said that having a prepaid cash card would make them "look cooler in front of their friends."

Private student loans are another story. Their rates are variable and can soar to nearly 20%. There are few restrictions on how much you can borrow, so you could easily rack up tens of thousands of dollars more than you can comfortably repay—and many, many young people have.

As mentioned earlier, this debt is yours until you repay it or death do you part. There are isolated, but disturbing, instances of despairing borrowers who took the latter route, committing suicide because they were overwhelmed by unpayable student debt.

What's more, some private student lenders aggressively pitch their products to young people without any mention that there's a better deal—federal student loans—that they should exhaust first before tapping into the private student loan market. The worst of

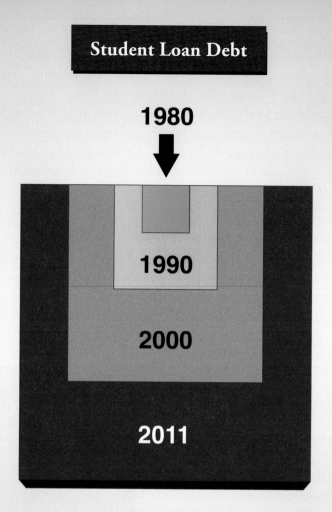

Student Loan Debt

1980

1990

2000

2011

Taken from: Occupy Posters, owposters.tumblr.com, no date. Original Source: Economic Research, Federal Reserve Bank of St. Louis.

the for-profit trade schools act as little more than pimps for these high-cost lenders.

So let's cut them off at the knees:

- Nobody under 21 can get a private student loan until they've applied for, and exhausted, federal student loans.
- Anyone who applies for a private student loan, or a federal graduate loan for that matter, should be warned that borrowing too much can be fatal to their financial lives, and that smart borrowers limit their education debt to no more than they expect to make their first year out of school.

No Zero-Down, Seventy-Two-Month Car Loans

Another area where people overdose on debt is buying cars. More than 80% of auto loans these days last longer than four years, according to car research site Edmunds.com, and one out of five new car buyers still owes money on his or her trade-in.

Long loans and the absence of down payments mean way too many drivers are upside-down on their vehicles, owing more than the cars are worth, which is potentially catastrophic for their finances.

We can help make sure young car buyers get off on a better foot by insisting they have some equity in whatever they drive and that the payments suit their incomes. We should impose rules that should be common sense for everyone. If people under 21 can't pay cash for a car, they should be required to:

- Make at least a 20% down payment on any car they finance.
- Limit financing to no more than four years.
- Have car payments equal to no more than 10% of their provable incomes.
- Will that condemn some teens to [low-priced] used Kias? Of course it will—and that's not the worst thing in the world. A Kia is a heck of a lot safer than some of the rattletraps we drove in my day, by gum. But more importantly, teenagers won't get accustomed to driving more car than they can afford, at least not while the ink is still fresh on their drivers' licenses.

EVALUATING THE AUTHOR'S ARGUMENTS:

Should the government help teens learn how to manage debt responsibly, as the author of this viewpoint argues, or should parents be responsible for teaching their children how to handle money, as the author of the next viewpoint, Sheryl Nance-Nash argues? Explain your answer, citing from the viewpoints.

Parents Can Do a Better Job of Teaching Their Kids About Money

"Parents are not making the grade as financial teachers for their children."

Sheryl Nance-Nash

Sheryl Nance-Nash is a contributor to *Forbes*, covering personal finance, with a focus on issues concerning families. In the following viewpoint, Nance-Nash reports on results from a 2012 survey in which parents and kids were interviewed about how successful parents are at teaching kids about money. The study found that although kids give parents a passing grade, there are many areas where parents can improve in teaching sound financial habits. Nance-Nash suggests parents take advantage of everyday opportunities to teach kids, model good behavior, and be open to sharing information about finances.

AS YOU READ, CONSIDER THE FOLLOWING QUESTIONS:
1. As stated by Nance-Nash, what percentage of parents are not always honest with kids about money-related items?
2. According to the T. Rowe Price survey cited by the author, what percentage of parents regularly set aside money to save and invest?
3. How does the author suggest parents improve as financial teachers?

P arents are not making the grade as financial teachers for their children, according to the 2012 Parents, Kids & Money survey from T. Rowe Price. For the first time kids were interviewed along with their parents. Kids ages 8–14 say they want to know more about money, particularly about saving and how to make money. However, while 76 percent of parents say they are having money conversations with their kids at least somewhat often, they aren't going far enough.

Pitfalls Parents Fall Into

For starters, parents aren't being honest. Nearly 80 percent say they are not always honest with their kids about money-related items, with 15 percent not telling the truth at least weekly. Most commonly, 43 percent of parents report not being honest about how worried they

Parents are more comfortable talking to their teens about bullying, smoking, and drugs than they are about financial matters, reports the author.

really are about money, 32 percent tell their children they can't afford something when they really can, and 27 percent withhold information about the family's true financial situation. Nearly a third of parents say they avoid talking with their kids about the family's current financial situation.

Parents just aren't comfortable talking finances. In fact, the survey revealed that they are more comfortable talking about bullying, drugs, and smoking than family finances or investing, and find talking about investing just as difficult as "the talk" about puberty and coming of age. Despite the fact that most parents are at least fairly well prepared to discuss basic financial concepts such as setting goals, the importance of saving, spending smartly, and the like, only half are teaching how to set a savings goal, 46 percent are teaching about spending and saving and fewer still are delving into inflation and investing.

Worse still, parents do not always set the best example when it comes to their own finances, with only half regularly setting aside money to save and invest, only 43 percent setting savings goals and only 24 percent ensuring investments are diversified.

Room for Improvement

Despite their shortcomings, on average, children gave their parents a B+ as financial teachers.

"While kids think their parents are good financial role models and do a good job teaching them about money, parental behavior suggests there's a lot of room for improvement. Parents don't need to be experts, but doing more to instill sound financial habits is crucial, especially given the uncertain financial future parents believe awaits their kids and if they don't want their kids to have the same financial regrets they do," said Stuart Ritter, a senior financial planner with T. Rowe Price, in a prepared statement.

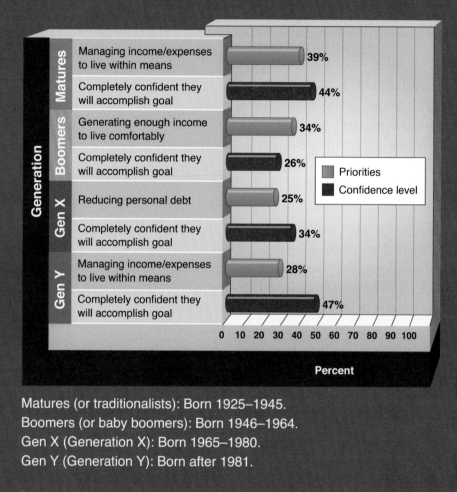

Financial Priorities and Optimism

		Priority/Goal	Percent
Matures		Managing income/expenses to live within means	39%
		Completely confident they will accomplish goal	44%
Boomers		Generating enough income to live comfortably	34%
		Completely confident they will accomplish goal	26%
Gen X		Reducing personal debt	25%
		Completely confident they will accomplish goal	34%
Gen Y		Managing income/expenses to live within means	28%
		Completely confident they will accomplish goal	47%

Legend: Priorities / Confidence level

Generation (y-axis) / Percent (x-axis: 0 10 20 30 40 50 60 70 80 90 100)

Matures (or traditionalists): Born 1925–1945.
Boomers (or baby boomers): Born 1946–1964.
Gen X (Generation X): Born 1965–1980.
Gen Y (Generation Y): Born after 1981.

Taken from: Joshua M. Brown. "Generational Differences in Attitudes Toward Money." March 15, 2011. www.thereformedbroker.com.

The survey had other interesting revelations:

Mom is the money guru. More than half of kids said they go to their moms first when they have a question about money, compared to 40 percent who go to their dads first.

Your kids are not stupid. Nearly half of parents say they don't always agree on money matters, and 42 percent of kids say they are aware of these disagreements.

Parents see bleak future for kids. Nearly 60 percent of parents feel it is likely that life exists on other planets, compared to the 26 percent who believe that Social Security will be available in its current form when their kids retire and the 39 percent who believe their children will become millionaires.

Breaking the Cycle

Keep it simple. Take advantage of everyday opportunities. There are plenty of chances, be it at the grocery store, while you're hitting up the ATM or planning the family vacation, to bring the value of the dollar, the importance of saving, of getting deals, of managing money properly.

Be a model money maven. It's not so much what you say, but what you do. If you're bouncing checks, always shopping, charging like there's no tomorrow, what do you think your children are going to do?

Share. You don't have to make the intimate details of your finances fodder for the dinner table, but do find a level of openness that you're comfortable with to talk about what you've learned about money.

According to the survey, many parents didn't get a strong financial foundation on finances growing up because their parents didn't talk to them about money. Don't let history repeat itself.

EVALUATING THE AUTHOR'S ARGUMENTS:

This viewpoint focuses on how parents can improve in teaching general financial literacy and sound money practices to their kids. How might a proactive approach like this impact the likelihood of a young person acquiring debt? How much influence does your parents' approach to money-related issues have on your own attitudes about money?

Teens Should Be Given Credit Cards at Age Sixteen

Roger Fortuna and Katie Escherich

"Make 16 the age you start teaching your child about financial independence and responsibility."

Roger Fortuna and Katie Escherich are reporters for ABC News. In the following viewpoint they provide advice from *Good Morning America* financial contributor Mellody Hobson. Hobson recommends getting teens a credit card at age sixteen that is tied to parents' accounts so that parents can monitor all transactions and ensure that their teen's bill gets paid on time. In addition, giving teens a credit card reduces the amount of cash teens need to carry and encourages them to see that credit is a privilege not to be abused.

AS YOU READ, CONSIDER THE FOLLOWING QUESTIONS:

1. According to an ABC News poll cited by the authors, what percentage of parents are opposed to giving kids a credit card?
2. As noted by Fortuna and Escherich, the average college senior with one credit card has about how much debt?
3. Why, according to the authors, does Hobson prefer charge cards to credit cards?

When should you give your kids a credit card? Should you wait until they're 18 and off to college? Or is younger better? This can be an explosive topic for parents, many of whom have very strong ideas about what's best for their teens when it comes to credit.

A new ABC News poll found that 71 percent of parents are opposed to giving kids a credit card before the age of 18, even one that has a restricted balance and is linked to a parent's account.

FAST FACT

A 2007 survey by marketing firm Starz for Kids found that 77 percent of kids aged eight to fourteen made online purchases, and 8 percent of them used their own credit cards.

"GMA" [*Good Morning America*] assembled a roundtable of moms and dads with children between 8 and 17, who were passionately divided about the topic. Some said children need to have access to credit to learn how to use it safely, while others were adamantly opposed to the idea.

Most parents agree that kids should learn to save and budget and should earn their own money. But when adults are struggling with their own credit along with the increasing and complex material needs of children, it can be difficult to decide when to help them get plastic.

"GMA" financial contributor Mellody Hobson has advice on how to handle this emotionally charged and divisive issue with your children.

What's the Appropriate Age?

Give Your Child a Credit Card at 16. Hobson disagrees with the majority in the ABC News poll, and advises getting your child a credit card linked to your account at 16. She thinks 18 is too late because, at that point, you no longer have total control over your child's spending and credit habits. Parents should look at 16 as a milestone age, she says. We already equate turning 16 with getting a driver's license, 18 with the right to vote and 21 with the right to drink. Make 16 the age you start teaching your child about financial independence and responsibility.

Benefits of Giving Your Teen a Card

You Can Monitor and Control Activity. A credit card can give you some control over your child's spending and credit management skills, especially before they go off to college, Hobson says. You can discuss with them the proper way to use credit before they get a card

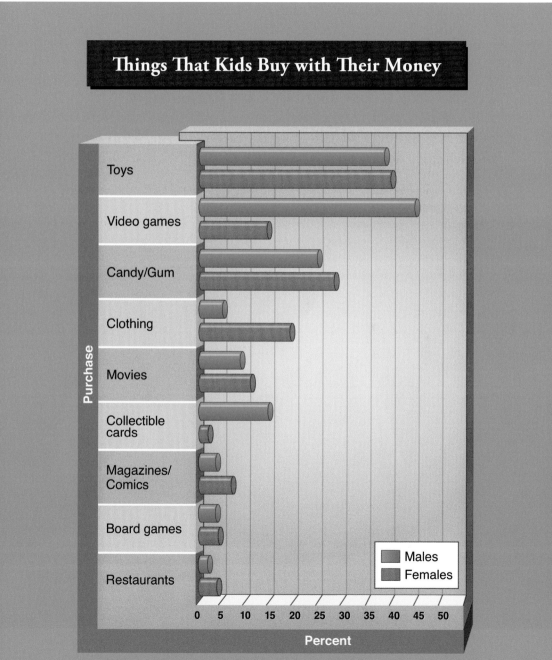

Things That Kids Buy with Their Money

Taken from: Experian Consumer Research. "What Do Kids Spend Their Money On?" 2007. www.marketingcharts.com.

of their own, kind of like credit with training wheels. You get to see all of your child's transactions in your monthly statement if they are an authorized user on your card, and you will be able to better recognize any impending issues and problems they might develop in the future.

Kids Won't Have to Carry a Lot of Cash. There's one other really big advantage to giving your 16-year-old a credit card, Hobson says. By giving your child a card, you're making sure they will not be carrying a ton of cash which can be very unsafe for them.

Teach Teens to Use a Credit Card Responsibly

Tell Kids the Card Is a Privilege. The average college senior with one credit card has over $4,100 in credit card debt, and Hobson says you definitely do not want your child to end up like that. When you

Financial experts say that teens should be given credit cards on a parent's account to better teach them about financial responsibility.

first get them a credit card, make sure you let them know that this is a privilege and you will be closely monitoring their use of the card.

Review, Discuss Bill Monthly. When you get the monthly credit card bill, review every single charge with your children. If you believe there are some unnecessary charges, then make sure you address it with them right away. Hobson is in favor of a new feature of the credit card act [Credit Card Accountability Responsibility and Disclosure Act of 2009, or Credit CARD Act] that requires bills to state the length of payments and the total interest charges you will incur if you only pay the minimum. She says it's a good way to teach teens about interest, and about the importance of paying their bill on time and in full.

Be a Good Role Model Yourself. Make sure you're demonstrating good credit card behavior yourself, Hobson says. Like everything else when it comes to parenting, you need to be a good role model. If you can't manage your own credit card, then no matter how hard you try, your teen will pick up your bad habits.

Have a Payment Plan. According to Hobson, another important thing to discuss with your teen is how they will pay for their charges. If they're not working, but are getting an allowance, Hobson recommends tying that allowance to their purchases. They should only be spending money that they have, otherwise they will really not have learned to manage their credit cards. And for big ticket items that you buy for them, they should have to pay you back with interest.

What Kind of Card Should You Get for Your Teen?

Get Card With Low Limit. Hobson says parents should give their children a credit card with a low limit, and find out whether you have the flexibility to change the limit at any time. For example, last year [2009] American Express launched an innovative benefit called "supps with limits." Your teen can get a supplemental card, and the parent has full control over the limit at any time.

Consider Charge Card or Debit Card. Hobson prefers charge cards, which differ from credit cards because they require you to pay your full balance each month. She also says that a debit card could be a good substitute for a credit card, because new laws have made opting-out of overdraft protection automatic, and your teen can only spend as much as they have.

Additional Tips

- In addition to getting a charge card with a low limit, make sure you only get your teen one credit card. Nobody needs more than one credit card, regardless of their age.
- The [Credit] CARD Act now automatically opts you out of overdraft protection. This is a very good thing. This so-called "protection" allows debit card users to overdraw their accounts in exchange for huge fees. Now you actually have to contact your card company and let them know you want this privilege. Do NOT opt in for this protection on your teen's debit card. If they purchase something that goes over their limit, and they do not have overdraft protection, then the transaction will be disallowed, which is exactly what you want.
- In addition to reviewing the bill with your teens, link their credit card to a site like Mint.com, which will help them easily track their spending, create a budget, and it will give them a good understanding of what exactly they are spending their money on.
- Make sure you review your credit report and your teen's credit reports from all three rating agencies annually. The only true place to get a free credit report is www.annualcreditreport.com.

EVALUATING THE AUTHOR'S ARGUMENTS:

After reading Roger Fortuna and Katie Escherich's viewpoint, what do you think is the appropriate age for a first credit card? Explain your answer.

Viewpoint

4

Debit Cards or Prepaid Cards Are a Better Alternative than Credit Cards for Teens

"'I will definitely encourage my son to get a credit card ... after he has proven to me that he can use a debit card without any issues.'"

Nancy Trejos

Nancy Trejos is the author of *Hot (Broke) Messes*, a book about young people and debt. In the following viewpoint she argues that teens should be taught financial responsibility but that debit and prepaid cards might be a better option than credit cards. She says these types of cards, which allow young people to spend money, not credit, can still teach the same lessons as credit cards without the risk to their credit score. In addition, Trejos notes, debit and prepaid cards can be used in most of the same retail situations as credit cards, so teens can learn the value of spending limits while shopping for their favorite purchases.

AS YOU READ, CONSIDER THE FOLLOWING QUESTIONS:
1. According to a 2007 Charles Schwab survey cited by Trejos, what percentage of teens know how to use a credit card?
2. According to that same survey, what percentage of teens understand credit card interest and fees?
3. What does the author recommend as a good limit for a debit or prepaid card for a teen?

S hashi Bellamkonda would like his 16-year-old daughter to get a credit card as soon as she is eligible.

Okay, that might sound kind of dangerous considering how much we have heard about teenagers (and let's face it, adults) getting into trouble with credit cards. Aren't there members of Congress who want to ban credit card companies from marketing to college students and young people in general? (The answer is yes.)

FAST FACT

The Mercator Advisory Group reports that in 2011 Americans loaded $42.1 million onto prepaid debit cards.

Bellamkonda, a 45-year-old Potomac resident who devises social media strategy for a company in Reston, [Virginia,] understands that. But he considers his daughter Mitali, a high school junior with good grades, responsible enough to handle credit. And he wants her to establish a credit history. After all, aren't we all supposed to take on a little bit of debt early in our lives in order to qualify for that good debt, such as a mortgage, later on in life?

There's another reason Bellamkonda wants his daughter to have a credit card. He wants it to be a learning experience. She's young enough now that if she has access to a credit card, he can monitor it. He'd rather she not have her first experience with credit when she is far away or living alone.

"Youngsters need to know that this is not a bottomless pit. So this may help educate her," he said. "Our prime focus should be on teaching children how to work with these various instruments."

Debit cards allow teens to spend money they have, not get credit, and so can help teach them how to use a credit card without incurring any debt.

If she makes mistakes, so be it, he said. "I'm not saying I want her to make mistakes, but if she does, it would be a good experience because we will be there to help her," he said.

Bellamkonda is wondering: Is this a good strategy? How should parents go about teaching their children about credit cards? Can his daughter even get a credit card? If so, would he be able to monitor the balance?

The credit card experts I consulted applauded Bellamkonda for teaching his daughter financial literacy early in life. Emily Peters, a personal finance expert for Credit.com, points to a 2007 Charles Schwab survey that showed that only 45 percent of teens know how to use a credit card. Even worse, just 26 percent of teens understood credit card interest and fees. "Shashi's doing the right thing by making sure she'll be prepared for her credit future," Peters said.

Using Credit Responsibly

But there are a few things Bellamkonda should consider before letting his daughter enter credit territory.

First of all, she might not even be able to get her own credit card. The recession has made financial institutions squeamish about giving unsecured loans, which is what credit cards are, to people with no established credit history. If she is able to get a credit card, he would probably have to be a co-signer, which means that if she mismanages the account, his credit score would be damaged along with hers.

Many personal finance experts would urge against letting your children get their own credit cards until they have a job that allows them to pay off their balances. Some even say they should wait until after college.

In the meantime, Bellamkonda has other, much better, options. If the goal is to get her used to dealing with plastic rather than cash, he can get her a debit card or a prepaid card with a low limit, say $250. Curtis Arnold, founder of CardRatings.com, said there are prepaid cards targeted specifically at teens, such as the Visa Buxx card. With such a card, Bellamkonda would be able to log in and monitor his daughter's spending online, Arnold said.

Arnold had his son, who just turned 18, start with a debit card. "I will definitely encourage my son to get a credit card when he gets in college after he has proven to me that he can use a debit card without any issues," he said.

Peters said Bellamkonda could also add his daughter as an authorized user on one of his existing accounts. That would allow him to monitor her spending. If she spends too much, he could pull the plug.

"That way, she'll gain the experience of using credit and start building her credit history but will not be legally responsible for her own account yet," Peters said.

Have a Long, Honest Talk

Of course, if Bellamkonda's credit is bad and he doesn't properly manage the card, his daughter's credit file would be damaged. But that does not appear to be the case. Whatever he decides to do, Bellamkonda should have a long, honest talk with his daughter.

Show her how carrying a balance and making minimum payments can result in finance charges far greater than the original purchase amount. CardRatings.com has an online calculator that illustrates this point. There are also good financial literacy resources at Jumpstart.org.

Bill Hardekopf, chief executive of LowCards.com, said parents should pull out their own credit card bills and talk their children through them. Explain the interest rate, minimum payments, grace period and finance charges. If they've had late fees or payment problems, they shouldn't hide them. "Use these as teaching examples," he said. "Getting a teenager a credit card while she lives in your home is a great teaching opportunity on finances."

EVALUATING THE AUTHOR'S ARGUMENTS:

Although Roger Fortuna and Katie Escherich in the preceding viewpoint recommend giving sixteen-year-olds credit cards, Nancy Trejos argues that debit cards and prepaid cards might be a better option. On the basis of your reading of the two viewpoints, which option do you think is the more effective?

Editorial: Higher Education Is Not a Bubble

"Buying a college education still yields a consistently good return on investment."

The Stanford Daily

The *Stanford Daily* is the student-run newspaper at Stanford University in California. In the following viewpoint the paper argues that higher education is still worth the cost. Although college tuition has soared in recent years, the author asserts that it is still worth borrowing for because of the higher salaries paid to college graduates. In addition, college graduates are much more likely to be employed than people who hold only high school diplomas. The author goes on to state that the cost of tuition has gone up because of the value placed on higher education in America and because of increasing demand by employers that job applicants have a college degree.

AS YOU READ, CONSIDER THE FOLLOWING QUESTIONS:
1. As stated in the *Stanford Daily*, by what percentage has the inflation-adjusted cost of college tuition increased since 1978?
2. According to the Bureau of Labor Statistics cited by the author, how much more money do people aged twenty-five and older make with a bachelor's degree than workers with just a high school diploma?
3. According to that same data, how much more per week do people with professional degrees make than people with just a diploma make?

The rising cost of higher education is one of the few features of American economic life to remain constant over the last few decades. Since 1978, the inflation-adjusted cost of college tuition has increased 650 percent; here at Stanford, the cost of tuition and room and board now stands at $52,341 per year. Despite many universities' (including Stanford's) efforts to increase need-based financial aid, the dramatic rise in the cost of education has left the average college senior with nearly $25,000 in debt. While skyrocketing student debt is cause for serious concern, investment in tuition should not be viewed as a bubble destined to pop. The bubble hypothesis implies that the costs of education now dwarf the benefits, a premise that the facts do not support. Higher education is a good investment for most students, especially those lucky enough to find themselves at Stanford.

The most recent data show that buying a college education still yields a consistently good return on investment. According to the Bureau of Labor Statistics, people aged 25 years or older with a bachelor's degree made $412 more each week and were half as likely to be unemployed in 2010 than those with only a high school diploma. Recipients of professional degrees did even better, making $984 more each week than people with only diplomas. On average, then, it only takes several years of work for an education to pay for itself in pure dollar terms.

To compare the bubble in higher education to the bubble in housing prices, then, you must believe that aggregate investment in college education does not confer economic value equivalent to tuition. Some have asserted that college degrees promise prestige or contacts, which only influence the distribution of wealth between those with degrees and those without, not the aggregate amount of wealth across society. With each college student convinced that *her* degree will entitle her to an inside track in the American economy, bubble proponents argue that college loans end up financing an expensive arms race for prestige, granting individual benefits at the cost of aggregate economic productivity.

Yet, this argument is also unconvincing. In a globalized labor market, American workers without degrees will continue to see their wages drop. As a society, we have pinned our hopes on a smarter economy, driven by brainpower rather than elbow grease. Until bubble theorists can explain how to train engineers, programmers, doctors, lawyers and other "thinking" professionals without sending them to places like

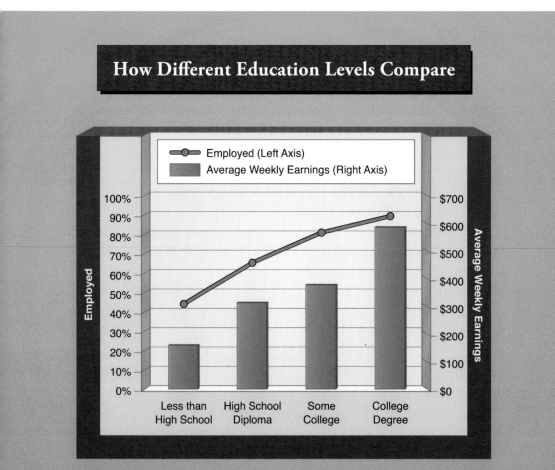

Taken from: Michael Greenstone and Adam Looney. "How Do Recent College Grads Really Stack Up? Employment and Earnings for Graduates of the Recession." The Brookings Institution, June 3, 2011.

Stanford, higher education will remain an excellent social investment. Beyond the individual benefits, there is something about Stanford that has consistently generated the exact kinds of economic juggernauts we need to thrive as a nation.

To students and to Americans, the last decade has shown that college is worth its price. Nonetheless, it is perfectly reasonable to inquire as to why that price has climbed so high. One theory holds that the rising cost of tuition simply reflects high demand for education running up against limited supply. To take this a step further, it is not the supply of education per se that is limited, but rather the supply of prestige.

Prestigious schools such as Stanford can maintain their prestige in only one way: by attracting the best students and faculty members. It is they who secure research grants, make donations and raise the pedigree of a university. Likewise, top students and brilliant researchers have a much greater incentive to attend or work for prestigious schools. Only in those environments can

they mingle with the best minds in their respective fields and feel confident that they will have the resources they need to conduct their work.

Unfortunately for tuition-paying families, prestige is not free. To stay ahead of their competition, universities are forced to build more state-of-the art labs and recreation centers, which inevitably drive up administrative costs. This effect applies not just to top-flight universities like Stanford, but also to 2nd and 3rd tier schools with nowhere near the name recognition we enjoy here on the Farm.

The ascendancy of prestige at the expense of tuition-paying students and parents has not been without benefits. Many of the intellectual and technological developments of our age would have been impossible were it not for the improvement and expansion of research and education facilities.

College tuition has increased 650 percent since 1978, so most students need to borrow money for college. Despite climbing costs, many believe college remains a worthwhile investment.

Some universities have already realized that families can only be squeezed so far. The expansion of need-based financial aid at Stanford in recent years is a prime example of the University's recognition of the need to enhance equity and access on campus.

As students, as alumni and as citizens, we must realize that rising tuition is not a burden imposed by some unseen nemesis, nor is it a bubble. So rest easy, Stanford: your education here has real and measurable benefits, both to you and to society as a whole.

EVALUATING THE AUTHOR'S ARGUMENTS:

After reading this viewpoint do you agree with the author that borrowing for college is worth the investment? Why or why not?

Viewpoint

6

Borrowing for College Is No Longer a Good Investment

"The younger generation ... appears to have mortgaged its future earnings in the form of student loan debt."

Alan Nasser and Kelly Norman

Alan Nasser is professor emeritus of political economy at the Evergreen State College in Washington State. Kelly Norman is a graduate student in public administration at Evergreen. In the following viewpoint Nasser and Norman argue that college degrees may no longer be worth the debt they bring. A lower percentage of college graduates receive job offers before graduation than ever in history. In addition, the interest rates on student loans make them difficult to pay back. Finally, as tuition increases, the number of students who must take out loans to pay for college grows.

AS YOU READ, CONSIDER THE FOLLOWING QUESTIONS:

1. As of 2010 what was the total student loan debt, as stated by the authors?
2. According to Nasser and Norman, by what percentage did the average debt levels for graduating seniors increase from 1994 to 2008?
3. According to the authors, by 2009 what percentage of college graduates who had applied for jobs had received an offer by graduation?

It was announced last summer [2010] that total student loan debt, at $830 billion, now exceeds total US credit card debt, itself bloated to the bubble level of $827 billion. And student loan debt is growing at the rate of $90 billion a year.

There are far fewer students than there are credit card holders. Could there be a student debt bubble at a time when college graduates' jobs and earnings prospects are as gloomy as they have been at any time since the Great Depression?

The data indicate that today's students are saddled with a burden similar to the one currently borne by their parents. Most of these parents have experienced decades of stagnating wages, and have only one asset, home equity. The housing meltdown has caused that resource either to disappear or to turn into a punishing debt load. The younger generation too appears to have mortgaged its future earnings in the form of student loan debt. . . .

Parallels with the Housing Bubble

The extraordinary growth of student debt paralleled the bubble years, from the beginnings of the dot.com bubble in the mid-1990s to the bursting of the housing bubble. From 1994 to 2008, average debt levels for graduating seniors more than doubled to $23,200, according to The Student Loan Project, a nonprofit research and policy organization. More than 10 percent of those completing their bachelor's degree are now saddled with over $40,000 in debt.

Are student loans as financially problematic as the junk mortgage securities still held by the biggest banks? That depends on how those loans were rated and the ability of the borrower to repay.

In the build-up to the housing crisis, the major ratings agencies used by the biggest banks gave high ratings to mortgage-backed securities that were in fact toxic. A similar pattern is evident in student loans.

The health of student loans is officially assessed by the "cohort-default rate," a supposedly reliable predictor of the likelihood that borrowers will default. But the cohort-default rate only measures the rate of defaults during the first two years of repayment. Defaults that occur after two years are not tracked by the Department of Education for institutional financial aid eligibility. Nor do government loans require credit checks or other types of regard for whether a student will be able to repay the loans.

There is about $830 billion in total outstanding federal and private student-loan debt. Only 40 percent of that debt is actively being repaid. The rest is in default, or in deferment (when a student requests temporary postponement of payment because of economic hardship), which means payments and interest are halted, or in forbearance [this type of relief may be granted if a loan is in default]. Interest on government loans is suspended during deferment, but continues to accrue on private loans.

As tuitions increase, loan amounts increase; private loan interest rates have reached highs of 20 percent. Add that to a deeply troubled economy and dismal job market, and we have the full trappings of a major bubble. As it goes with contemporary bubbles, when the loans go into default, taxpayers will be forced to pick up the tab, since just about all loans made before July 2010 are backed by the federal government.

Of course the usual suspects are among the top private lenders: Citigroup, Wells Fargo and JP Morgan-Chase.

Financial Aid and Subprime Lending

A higher percentage of students enrolled at private, for-profit ("proprietary") schools hold education debt (96 percent) than students at public colleges and universities or students attending private non-profits.

Two out of every five students enrolled at proprietary schools are in default on their education loans 15 years after the loans were issued. In spite of this high extended default rate, for-profit colleges are in no danger of losing their access to federal financial aid because, as we have seen, the Department of Education does not record defaults after the first two years of repayment.

Nor have the disturbing findings of recent Congressional hearings on the recruitment techniques of proprietary colleges jeopardized these schools' access to federal funds. The hearings displayed footage from an undercover investigation showing admissions staff at proprietary schools using recruitment techniques explicitly forbidden by the National Association of College Admissions Counselors. Admissions and enrollment employees are also shown misrepresenting the costs of an education, the graduation and employment rates of students, and the accreditation status of institutions.

These deceptions increase the likelihood that graduates of for-profits will have special difficulties repaying their loans, since the majority enrolled at these schools are low-income students.

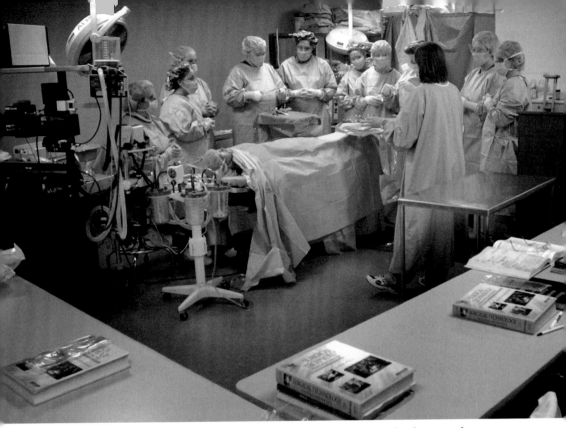

A class is held at a for-profit university. The author informs the reader that two of every five students enrolled at proprietary schools are in default on their loans fifteen years after taking out the loan.

A credit score is not required for federal loan eligibility. Neither is information regarding income, assets, or employment. Borrowing is still encouraged in the face of strong evidence that the likelihood of default is high.

Loaning money to anyone without prime qualifications was "subprime lending" during the ballooning of the housing bubble, when banks were enticing otherwise ineligible candidates to buy houses they could not afford.

Shouldn't easy lending without adequate credit checks to college students with insecure credit also be considered "subprime lending"? . . .

The Private Lenders: Securitization as Usual

The two largest holders of student loans are SLM Corp (SLM) and Student Loan Corp (STU), a subsidiary of Citigroup. SLM—Sallie Mae—was originated as a Government Sponsored Enterprise (GSE) in 1972. The idea was to prime it for eventual privatization. In 2002 Sallie Mae shed its GSE status and became a subsidiary of the Delaware-chartered publicly traded holding company SLM Holding Corporation. Finally, in 2004 the company officially terminated its ties to the federal government.

As the nation's largest single private provider of student loan funding, SLM has to date lent to more than 31 million students. In 2009 it lent approximately $6.3 billion in private loans and between $5.5 billion and $6 billion in 2010.

In the 1990s, well before its full privatization, Sallie's operations were increasingly swept into the financialization of the economy. It jumped whole hog onto the securitization bandwagon, lumping together and repackaging a large portion of its loans and selling them as bonds to investors. SLM created and marketed its own species of asset-backed securitized student loans, Student Loan Asset Backed Securities (SLABS). When derivatives trading went through the roof following the 1998 repeal of Glass-Steagal [a law from the 1930s limiting banks' affiliations with securities firms], increasingly diverse tranches [types or classes] of Sallie-Mae-backed SLABS entered the market. The company is now also buying and selling the obligations of state and nonprofit educational-loan agencies.

> **FAST FACT**
>
> Two-thirds of college seniors graduated with outstanding student loans in 2010, with an average debt of about twenty-five thousand dollars, according to the Institute for College Access and Success.

Student loans were included in the same securities that are blamed for the triggering of the financial crisis, and financial products containing these same student loans continue to be traded to this day. The health of these tranches and securities is, as we have seen, highly suspect.

SLM's risk was minimized as long as the feds guaranteed its loans. But as part of last March's [2009] health care legislation, starting in July 2010 federally subsidized education loans were no longer available to private lenders. What do education loans have to do with health care? Since the government took federal loan originations in-house, making them available only through the Department of Education, it no longer has to pay hefty fees (acting as the guarantee) to private banks. The [Barack] Obama administration expects to save $68 billion between now and 2020. $19 billion of this will be used to pay for the $940 billion health care bill.

While there is scant relief for student borrowers, private banks manage to survive apparent setbacks just fine. SLM will do quite well despite the withdrawal of government backing. The company anticipated the change in government lending policy by executing an ingenious trick as a borrower. Early last year it made its insurance subsidiary a member of the Federal Home Loan Bank of Des Moines, which agreed to lend to big-borrower SLM at the extraordinary rate of .23 percent. And anyhow, subsidized loans are almost always insufficient to cover the entire cost of a college degree. For a while the student gets to enjoy the benefits of a government loan. Interest rates are lower and during deferment interest does not accrue. But eventually many students must also take out a private loan, usually in larger amounts and with higher interest rates which continue to mount during deferment.

The Worst-Case Scenario: Going Bankrupt

Credit card and even gambling debts can be discharged in bankruptcy. But ditching a student loan is virtually impossible, especially once a collection agency gets involved. Although lenders may trim payments, getting fees or principals waived seldom happens.

[On February 13, 2010,] the *Wall Street Journal* ran a revealing report on the kinds of situations that can lead to financial catastrophe for a student borrower. Here is an excerpt illustrating the toll that forced indebtedness can take on the student borrower:

> When Michelle Bisutti, a 41-year-old family practitioner [physician] in Columbus, Ohio, finished medical school in 2003, her student-loan debt amounted to roughly $250,000. Since then, it has ballooned to $555,000.
>
> It is the result of her deferring loan payments while she completed her residency, default charges and relentlessly compounding interest rates. Among the charges: a single $53,870 fee for when her loan was turned over to a collection agency.

Although Bisutti's debt load is unusual, her experience having problems repaying isn't. Emmanuel Tellez's mother is a laid-off factory worker, and $120 from her $300 unemployment checks is garnished to pay the federal student loan she took out for her son.

By the time Tellez graduated in 2008, he had $50,000 of his own debt in loans issued by SLM. . . . In December, he was laid off from his $29,000-a-year job in Boston and defaulted [on the loan].

Heather Ehmke of Oakland, Calif., renegotiated the terms of her subprime mortgage after her home was foreclosed. But even after filing for bankruptcy, she says she couldn't get Sallie Mae, one of her lenders, to adjust the terms on her student loan. After 14 years with patches of deferment and forbearance, the loan has increased from $28,000 to more than $90,000. Her monthly payments jumped from $230 to $816. Last month, her petition for undue hardship on the loans was dismissed.

The First Austerity Generation's Job Prospects

Most of those affected by the meltdown of 2008 had completed their education and were either employed or retired. The student loan debt bubble signals a generation that enters the [world] of paid work cursed with what is more likely than not to be a life of permanent indebtedness and low wages.

The current cohort of indebted students will face earnings prospects far poorer than what job seekers could expect during the period of the longest wave of sustained economic growth and the highest wages in US history, 1949–1973. The present generation will experience the indefinite extension of [Ronald] Reagan-to-Obama low wage neoliberalism [where free trade, privatization, and reduced access to social services are favored].

According to the National Association of Colleges and Employers more than 50 percent of all 2007 college graduates who had applied for a job had received an offer by graduation day. In 2008, that percentage tumbled to 26 percent, and to less than 20 percent in 2009. And a college education has been producing diminishing returns. For while a college degree does tend to correlate with a relatively high income, during the last eight to ten years the median income of highly educated Americans has been declining.

Every two years the Bureau of Labor Statistics [BLS] issues projections of how many jobs will be added in the key occupational categories over the next ten years. The projected future jobs picture indicates that the grim employment situation is not merely a temporary reflection of the current, unusually severe downturn. But you miss this if you get your news only from mainstream sources. The *New York Times*'s report on the most recent BLS projections, released in December 2009, paints an unduly optimistic picture of future employment opportunities. Here is how a misleading report can be produced without falsifying the facts:

BLS releases two job projections, on the Fastest Growing Occupations and on Occupations With the Largest Job Growth. The *Times* focuses on the former, where the two fastest growing occupations, biomedical engineers and network systems and data communications analysts, require a college degree. The *Times* echoes BLS's

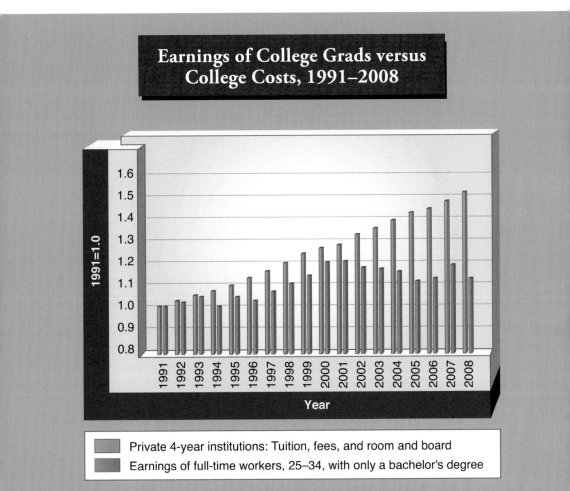

Earnings of College Grads versus College Costs, 1991–2008

Private 4-year institutions: Tuition, fees, and room and board

Earnings of full-time workers, 25–34, with only a bachelor's degree

Taken from: Michael Mandel. "Earnings of Young College Grads vs College Costs." *Businessweek*, September 12, 2010.

comment that occupations requiring postsecondary (a bachelor's degree or higher) credentials will grow fastest. This is redolent of the ideology of the "New Economy": the US is turning into a society of professionals and knowledge workers, and the key to success in this upgraded economy is a college education.

But we need more information, about the degree requirements of the total number of job categories listed in both projections, and about the number of new jobs expected to materialize in each projection.

Of the total jobs listed, only one of five require a postsecondary degree. By far the fastest growing category is biomedical engineers, projected to grow 72.02 percent, from 16,000 in 2008 to 27, 600 in 2018. That's 11,600 new jobs. Is that a lot? Well, compared to what? The percentage figure, 72.02, is high, but what about the number of new jobs? Let's compare that Fastest Growing occupation with retail salespersons, the occupation fifth down on the Largest Growth list. Retail sales workers will grow by a mere 8.35 percent. But that amounts to almost 375,000 new jobs, an increase from 4,489,000 jobs in 2008 to 4,863,000 jobs in 2018. Compare that to the 11,600 new jobs at the top of the Fastest Growing list. Just do the simple math on all the categories on both lists: the great majority of new jobs will be low-paying.

This is a nation of knowledge workers? Most new jobs will offer the kind of wage we would expect from an economy in which, according to one of Obama's most repeated mantras, "we" will "consume less and export more". BLS avers as much when it projects that fewer than 12 million of the 51 million "job openings due to growth and replacement needs" will require a bachelor's degree.

Our first austerity generation will be in debt to its teeth and stuck with low-wage work. The relative penury will require more debt still. Michael Hudson calls this debt peonage. Not to sound like a broken record, but we need to get off our asses and begin taking seriously political organization that goes beyond the ballot box. Not that voting is entirely irrelevant. We can imitate those activists—bankers, hedge fund managers, and corporate CEOs—who stoutly refuse to support, financially or at the ballot box, candidates who will not give them what they want. These days, those folks always get what they want. Liberals and too many Leftists have not learned that elementary political lesson.

Student Loans Should Be Eligible for Discharge Through Bankruptcy

"It's 'unfair,' ... for other loans ... to be forgiven in bankruptcy proceedings while student loans are not."

Jennifer Epstein

Jennifer Epstein is currently the White House reporter at Politico.com, a website that focuses on national politics. In the following viewpoint she argues that student loans should be eligible for discharge through bankruptcy. The average student loan debt in the United States has never been higher, especially private student loans. Except for the most extreme situations, student loans are no longer eligible for clearance through bankruptcy, but several lawmakers are intent on changing that. Epstein reports that unclear definitions of "undue hardship," the only circumstance under which loan borrowers can file bankruptcy, makes it more challenging.

Jennifer Epstein, "Rethinking Bankruptcy and Student Loans," *Inside Higher Ed,* September 24, 2009. Reproduced by permission.

1. As stated by the author, what do federal student loans for independent undergraduates in the last two years of study top out at?
2. According to the Institute for College Access and Success, as cited by Epstein, what percentage of all four-year undergraduate college students have student loans?
3. In what year was the bankruptcy code revised to make it nearly impossible to file against student loan debt, according to the author?

A s Congress and the White House move to alter bankruptcy code to make it more equitable to consumers, a House subcommittee began a reconsideration Wednesday [September 23, 2009,] of how bankruptcy law treats private student loan debt.

Rep. Steve Cohen (D-Tenn.), chair of the House Judiciary Subcommittee on Commercial and Administrative Law, held a hearing to initiate legislation reversing a 2005 change in federal bankruptcy law that, he said, gave private student loan lenders a "favorable, unusual" advantage over borrowers, as well as in comparison to the issuers of most other kinds of consumer loans. "Hopefully it'll be bipartisan and if not, you know, we'll just have to forge ahead and do what's right."

After the hearing, he formally announced plans to file legislation to "give private student loan borrowers more equitable treatment during the bankruptcy process."

Rep. George Miller (D-Calif.), chairman of the House Education and Labor Committee, hailed the drafting of new legislation as meeting "a growing need to protect students from financially riskier private student loans and predatory lending practices," especially with rising college costs and an unemployment rate approaching 10 percent.

The subcommittee's senior Republican, Rep. Trent Franks of Arizona, seemed receptive to some reform of the private student loan industry, but cautioned that if the bill passed last week "isn't the death knell of private student lending, ending the favorable treatment student loans receive under bankruptcy code certainly could be."

Bankruptcy law bars virtually all borrowers from discharging their private student loan debt, even as most other forms of consumer debt—including auto loans, credit card debt and mortgages—can be discharged through bankruptcy proceedings. The only exceptions are made in cases of "undue hardship."

Though federally guaranteed student loans usually can't be canceled in bankruptcy cases either, they do come with fixed interest rates, flexible payment plans and other consumer protections that generally make them less onerous for borrowers, said Lauren Asher, president of the Berkeley, Calif.–based Institute for College Access and Success. "Private student loans are one of the riskiest ways to pay for college," she said, adding that the loans "are not financial aid any more than using a credit card to pay for tuition or books is financial aid."

Even so, students are turning to the loans to make up the gap between federal student loans (which top out at $12,500 per academic year for independent undergraduates in the last two years of study) and the ever-rising costs of tuition and fees at American colleges and universities. According to calculations by Asher's organization, two-thirds of all graduates of four-year colleges have student loans, averaging $23,200 in federal and private loans, and a third of students who earned a bachelor's degree in 2007–8 took out a private student loan during their time in college.

Fourteen percent of all U.S. undergraduates took out a private student loan in that academic year, up from 4 percent in 2003–4.

Rep. Danny Davis (D-Ill.) testified at the hearing on behalf of the Congressional Black Caucus's Community Reinvestment Task Force, which he co-chairs, and expressed particular concern for African-American students who, he said, "were statistically more likely to borrow private student loans," at a rate of 17 percent.

Last year [2008], as the House voted to reauthorize the Higher Education Act, Davis proposed an amendment that would have allowed borrowers filing for bankruptcy to discharge their pri-

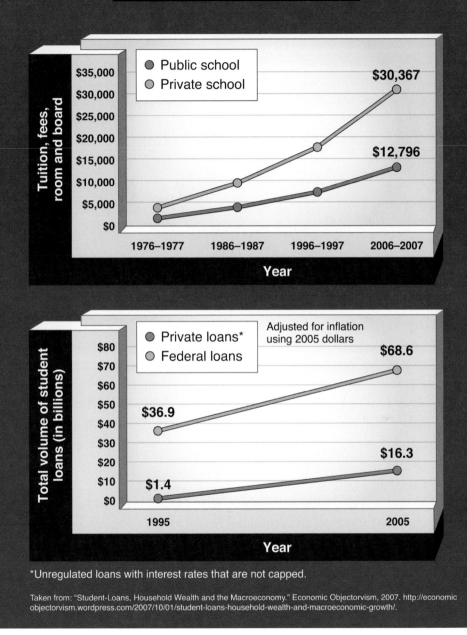

Student Loan Increases

Public school
Private school

Tuition, fees, room and board

$35,000
$30,000
$25,000
$20,000
$15,000
$10,000
$5,000
$0

1976–1977 1986–1987 1996–1997 2006–2007

Year

$30,367
$12,796

Private loans*
Federal loans

Adjusted for inflation using 2005 dollars

Total volume of student loans (in billions)

$80
$70
$60
$50
$40
$30
$20
$10
$0

1995 2005

Year

$68.6
$36.9
$16.3
$1.4

*Unregulated loans with interest rates that are not capped.

Taken from: "Student-Loans, Household Wealth and the Macroeconomy." Economic Objectorvism, 2007. http://economic objectorvism.wordpress.com/2007/10/01/student-loans-household-wealth-and-macroeconomic-growth/.

vate student loans as part of that process, so long as the loan had required repayment for at least five years. The measure failed in a 236 to 179 vote. Cohen's bill will probably be modeled after Davis's amendment.

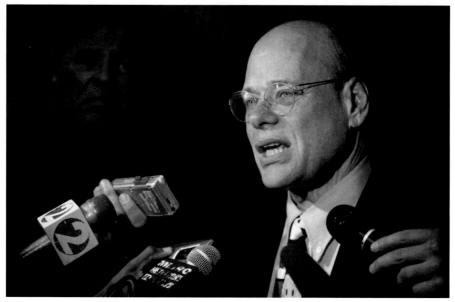

In 2005 Tennessee representative Steve Cohen filed legislation to "give private student loan borrowers more equitable treatment during the bankruptcy process."

Facing Bankruptcy

Over the course of earning a bachelor's degree, a student at a particularly pricey institution receiving little or no grant aid could end up borrowing $100,000 or more in private loans, said Brett Weiss, a consumer bankruptcy lawyer who testified on behalf of the National Association of Consumer Bankruptcy Attorneys and the National Consumer Law Center. It's "unfair," he said, for other loans of that magnitude, like mortgages, to be forgiven in bankruptcy proceedings while student loans are not.

J. Douglas Cuthbertson, a lawyer who represents financial institutions in federal consumer financial litigation for the McLean, Va.-based law firm Miles & Stockbridge, warned of "debtors filing for bankruptcy almost solely on student loans," as was sometimes the case before 1976, when Congress barred discharge of student loans within five years of college graduation. A 1990s change to bankruptcy code made the minimum seven years, and the 2005 code revision made it all but impossible to have student loan debt canceled.

Franks and Rep. Howard Coble (R-N.C.), the two only members of their party at the hearing, voiced support for Cuthbertson's argument, the same one that has been used by Republicans whenever changes to bankruptcy law have been considered.

But Weiss cited a 1970s study by the Government Accountability Office that found that less than 1 percent of all matured student loans had been discharged in bankruptcy and dismissed Republican concerns about widespread manipulation of the bankruptcy code.

The notion that "people who view bankruptcy as an easy option . . . is so far from the reality, it's just absolutely dead wrong," he said. "Student loans are not primary factors for bankruptcy filings. Student loans are sort of in the mix. . . . People very, very rarely file for bankruptcy because of a student loan."

Defining "Undue Hardship"

The only chance borrowers have to discharge their private student loans during bankruptcy proceedings comes by being able to demonstrate "undue hardship," a term that has not been concretely defined by Congress and is up for varied interpretations by bankruptcy judges.

Rafael I. Pardo, an associate professor at the Seattle University School of Law who has done extensive studies on student loans and their discharge in bankruptcy, called on Congress "to clarify the undue hardship standard."

Courts generally go through long investigations to determine whether debtors have faced exceptional challenges, such as physical or mental disabilities, a lack of job skills or an absence of future earning potential. Final rulings are up to the discretion of judges, Asher of the Institute for College Access and Success said, and much more likely to happen with the benefit of "a high-priced attorney."

All four experts who testified voiced support for Congress to create its own definition of "undue hardship," which could be easily used to evaluate all bankruptcy cases involving student loans.

Democrats and Republicans on the subcommittee were all receptive to the formulation of a definition.

EVALUATING THE AUTHOR'S ARGUMENTS:

Do you agree with Jennifer Epstein that student loans should be discharged in bankruptcy? Why or why not?

Viewpoint

8

Student Loans Should Not Be Eligible for Discharge Through Bankruptcy

"I believe that making student loans dischargeable in bankruptcy is not a good idea."

Alfred Edmond Jr.

In the following viewpoint Alfred Edmond Jr., the editor at large of *Black Enterprise*, argues that student loans should not be eligible for discharge through bankruptcy. He insists that allowing them to be dismissed would encourage more students to take out loans frivolously and maybe even with no intention of repaying them. In addition, he believes that it would limit the number of student loans available to students, especially African Americans. He encourages young people to work hard to pay back their loans and to consider them a good debt that will help them in the future.

Alfred Edmond Jr., "Student Loans Should Not Be Discharged in Bankruptcy," *Black Enterprise,* December 14, 2010. Copyright © 2010 by Earl G. Graves Publishing Co. Inc. All rights reserved. Reproduced by permission.

1. If passed, what does the author say will be the result of the Private Student Loan Bankruptcy Fairness Act of 2010?
2. What law made it nearly impossible to dismiss student loans through bankruptcy, as stated by Edmond?
3. Why does the author refer to student loan debt as "good debt"?

Recently, my colleague Sheiresa Ngo, multimedia content producer for consumer affairs for *Black Enterprise*, made a quite reasonable case for her belief that private student loans should be dischargeable in bankruptcy. Her post, "Opinion: Student Loans Should Be Discharged in Bankruptcy," generated lots of comments, mostly in support of her proposal, which could become reality if the proposed Private Student Loan Bankruptcy Fairness Act of 2010 becomes law. As a father of a daughter who is struggling to pay back her student loans since graduating from college in 2005, I absolutely understand the challenges many Americans, and Black Americans in particular, face in coping with the burden of student loans.

However, I believe making student loans dischargeable in bankruptcy is not a good idea, and would really backfire on students whose families don't have the means to front the cost of college tuition and/or who are not able to compete for athletic or academic scholarships or secure enough financial aid to cover education costs. Once you make student loans from banks dischargeable in bankruptcy, they will immediately become unavailable to most students (and probably all students of modest means) or available only under the most onerous terms, including much higher fees and interest rates. In short, it would be even harder to pay the loans back. And it would be costly and difficult, if not impossible, to prevent abuses of such a policy, i.e., people generating student loan debt with no intention of paying it back. In fact, it could take the current student loan crisis and make it immeasurably worse, as people, out of either ignorance or laziness, forgo the challenge of securing scholarships, grants and other preferable forms of aid. They could end up borrowing more money than wise or necessary for college, when the better option would be to go to an in-state school, a public university or a two-year college and then finishing up at a four-year school. "After all," they'll mistakenly believe, "if I can't pay it back, I'll just file for bankrutptcy protection."

Bankruptcy Is Difficult to Obtain

Actually, the last thing a young person needs on their credit report coming out of college (especially if they are unemployed or under-employed) is a bankruptcy filing—the financial event with the worst possible impact on your credit scores, far worse than the impact of defaulting on a student loan. Remember, everyone from potential employers to apartment renters will look at those credit reports, making it more difficult for a young person to land a job, get affordable car insurance or rent an apartment, as all of these are impacted by your credit worthiness. And many recent college graduates have weak credit histories to start with, as they're in the early stages of their careers (with incomes to match—if they're lucky enough to have landed a job) and have shorter credit histories.

It's important to remember that bankruptcy is far from an easy way out of financial woes. The Bankruptcy Abuse Prevention and Consumer Protection Act (BAPCPA) of 2005 made sweeping changes to American bankrupty laws, with provisions explicitly designed by the bill's Congressional sponsors to make it more difficult for people to file for bankruptcy. Those who want to file must jump through a variety of hoops, including mandatory credit counseling and a means test based on a comparison of their monthly income versus the median income in their state. And remember, filing for bankruptcy costs money in the form of legal fees, court costs and other expenses—which must be paid even if the bankruptcy filing is rejected.

Finally, here's an unpopular and inconvenient truth: While there are many who have been legitimately unable to keep up with student loan payments, I suspect that there are at least as many people who just

Student Loan Interest Rate Increases

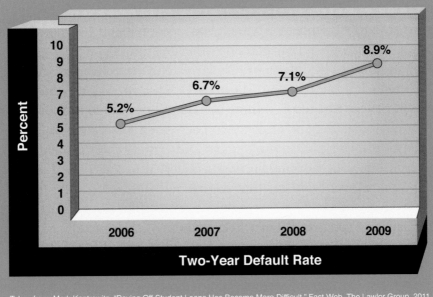

Taken from: Mark Kantrowitz. "Paying Off Student Loans Has Become More Difficult." Fast Web, The Lawlor Group, 2011.

did not make such payments a priority, even after they gained employment. I had student loans to repay when I graduated from college back in 1983, which also happened to be during a recession. (My mother, a single parent of four dependent on public assistance, was unable to contribute anything toward my college costs.) After graduation, I slept on a sofa bed in my mother's living room during the four months it took me to find two low-paying, part-time jobs. When I finally landed a full-time entry-level job in Brooklyn, N.Y., I shared an apartment with a college classmate who also went unemployed for 6 months after graduation. I went without furniture (sleeping on a mattress on the floor and later securing second-hand furniture donated by a relative), relied on public transportation, bought no new clothes for nearly two years and rarely spent money at restaurants, clubs or the movies.

My goal: To pay back my student loans as quickly as possible. My motivation: I'd worked hard to earn my degree, and I wanted to own it outright. I knew up front that a college education is not free—that's why I pursued scholarships, applied for financial aid and took out student loans in the first place. After rent, utilities and food, paying off my student loan was my top priority. (Some months, it came ahead of spending on food). As a result, I did just that in less than three years (saving a bundle on interest), despite never earning more than $15,000 annually during that time and with no help from my parents or other family members. To me it was a no-brainer. I had no wife, no kids, no mortgage, no car note, no other major obligations—just me. Why shouldn't I be able to pay back the loan once I started working?

Though it's important to borrow as little money as possible to toward college financing, if there is any kind of debt to be stuck with, it's student loan debt. It's called good debt for a reason: you still have a better chance of gaining employment and earning more money during the course of your working life with a college degree than without one. The catch is, once you get that degree and start generating income, you have to start paying that money back as soon as you can, even if you have to make painful sacrifices to do it. Unfortunately, too many recent newly minted graduates put establishing a lifestyle ahead of paying their student loans after finding employment.

Americans struggling with student loan debt definitely need relief, including banks, the government, the private sector, and colleges and universities working together to come up with more creative ways for people to pay off their student loan debt. God knows, as a parent of a college graduate struggling with student loan debt and three other children in various stages of college, I need all the help I can get—we all do. However, bankruptcy is not the answer.

EVALUATING THE AUTHOR'S ARGUMENTS:

The author of this viewpoint included a personal anecdote of how he paid off his student loans in the 1980s. Did his anecdote bolster his argument? Do you think his success story could apply to students today? Why or why not?

Chapter 2

What Are the Best Ways to Manage Consumer Debt?

Managing debt is something every teen needs to learn how to do.

The Credit Card Reform Act Has Been Effective

Jennifer Liberto

Jennifer Liberto is a senior writer at CNNMoney.com. In the following viewpoint she argues that the Credit Card Reform Act of 2009 has largely been successful. She follows White House official Elizabeth Warren's lead in praising the measures that have resulted in consumers' paying fewer late fees, including over-limit fees and interest rate hikes. Also, the act requires credit card companies to reveal to cardholders just how much the credit costs and how long it will take to pay off their debts. Unfortunately, according to Liberto, the act has caused a limit in credit availability and has driven up the cost of running a line of credit.

"After the new laws went into effect, only 2% of credit card accounts were subject to rate hikes, down from 15%."

AS YOU READ, CONSIDER THE FOLLOWING QUESTIONS:
1. As stated by Liberto, what is the function of the Consumer Financial Protection Bureau?
2. According to a study by the Office of the Comptroller and Currency, as cited by the author, what percentage of credit card accounts were subject to rate hikes after the new credit card law went into effect?
3. According to the same study, by what percentage did the total amount of late fees drop?

Jennifer Liberto, "Bank Critic Praises Credit Card Companies," CNNMoney.com, February 22, 2011. Reproduced by permission.

Whi te House official Elizabeth Warren, best known for her outspoken criticism of the banking industry, praised that same group during a Tuesday [February 22, 2011,] conference on the one-year anniversary of the credit card laws [Credit Card Accountability Responsibility and Disclosure Act of 2009, or Credit CARD Act].

A year after new credit card laws curbed interest rate hikes and forced new disclosures, consumers are paying fewer late fees and have a better understanding of what their cards cost, according to a federal study.

White House official Elizabeth Warren praised the Credit CARD Act of 2009 that has allowed consumers to suffer fewer late fees and interest rate hikes.

"The data we have assembled indicates that much of the industry has gone further than the law requires in curbing repricing and over-limit fees," Warren said. "Leaders in the industry deserve credit for moving in the right direction."

Warren is the [Barack Obama] administration's point person for setting up the Consumer Financial Protection Bureau, an independent agency funded by the Federal Reserve and charged with regulating credit cards and mortgages.

Warren also said that more needs to be done, especially when it comes to "clarifying price and risk and making it easier for consumers to make direct product comparisons."

> **FAST FACT**
>
> According to the Center for Responsible Lending, the Credit CARD Act can save cardholders as much as two dollars for every dollar paid above the minimum monthly payment.

That's where the consumer bureau will step in. But that bureau has faced a new round of scrutiny by House Republicans [GOP] intent on slashing spending and shrinking government.

Improvements for Consumers

Last year [in 2010], new laws took effect that made it more difficult for banks and credit card issuers to hike a cardholder's interest rates based on things like missing one payment or paying an unrelated bill late. Congress also required credit cards to disclose how long it would take to pay down credit cards making minimum payments.

A study conducted by the Office of Comptroller of the Currency found that after the new laws went into effect, only 2% of credit card accounts were subject to rate hikes, down from 15% of accounts prior to the new laws.

Other findings in the study include:

- The total amount of late fees collected dropped by more than half from $901 million in January 2010 to $427 million in November 2010.
- The number of accounts hit with over-the-limit fees, for charges beyond the credit limit, "virtually disappeared," the report said, dropping from 12% of credit card accounts to 1%.

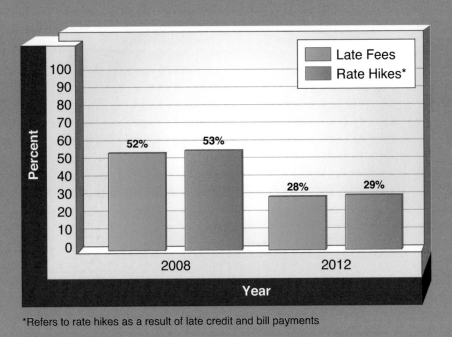

Households Reporting Accrual of Late Fees and Imposition of Rate Hikes, 2008 and 2012

Late Fees
Rate Hikes*

Percent

2008: 52%, 53%
2012: 28%, 29%

Year

*Refers to rate hikes as a result of late credit and bill payments

Taken from: Amy Traub. "The Credit CARD Act: It's Working." Demos, May 22, 2012. www.demos.org/data-byte /credit-card-fees-penalties-associatied-late-payment.

Banking industry representatives said they have few complaints. "It really gives people a good understanding of the cost of credit," said Scott Talbott, senior lobbyist for the Financial Services Roundtable, a bank lobbying group.

The Downside of the Law

But the American Bankers Association [ABA] maintains the law did put a crunch on the availability and cost of credit.

"Recent data indicates that the cost of credit and its availability have been negatively impacted by the Act, particularly for working class Americans, many of whom have been edged out of the marketplace or are facing higher upfront rates and tougher credit terms," said ABA senior vice president and chief attorney Kenneth J. Clayton.

The conference on credit cards comes on the heels of several days of new criticism lobbed against the consumer bureau by House Republicans. During a debate over cutting this year's budget, GOP lawmakers railed against the agency, arguing they should have more control over its operations and funding.

EVALUATING THE AUTHOR'S ARGUMENTS:

Should the US government restrict credit card companies' lending practices? Explain, using Jennifer Liberto's viewpoint to support your argument.

The Credit Card Reform Act Has Limitations

Tony Mecia

"[The Credit CARD Act] is a significant first step, but it doesn't fix everything."

In the following viewpoint Tony Mecia, a regular contributor to CreditCards.com and the *Weekly Standard,* argues that the Credit Card Accountability Responsibility and Disclosure Act of 2009, or Credit CARD Act, does not fully protect consumers from credit card companies. Although the new law limits the amount of fees charged to cardholders exceeding credit limits and making late payments, other fees, such as for not using the card regularly or for charging less than a specified amount, are still being leveled at consumers. Also, interest rates can be upped for new purchases, credit card limits can be lowered at any time, and even long-existing accounts can be closed.

AS YOU READ, CONSIDER THE FOLLOWING QUESTIONS:

1. To what types of credit cards does the Credit CARD Act of 2009 apply, according to Mecia?
2. According to the act, as cited by the author, how many days' notice must banks give to consumers before they raise interest rates?
3. According to a January 2010 survey by the National Small Business Association cited by Mecia, what percentage of respondents said that rates and terms of conditions on credit cards had worsened in the last five years?

Despite a sweeping credit card law that adds protections for consumers this month [February 2010], card issuers will still largely remain free to set the terms of your account in crucial areas such as interest rates and fees.

As a result, consumer groups figure that complaints about card issuers are likely to continue even after the bulk of the law takes effect Feb. 22.

"A huge step has been made to protect consumers from the worst tricks and traps," says Lauren Bowne, staff attorney with Consumers Union. "It is a significant first step, but it doesn't fix everything."

The law—the Credit CARD Act of 2009 [Credit Card Accountability Responsibility and Disclosure Act of 2009]—regulates how card issuers handle specific issues in areas including billing, disclosure, youth marketing and introductory offers. But companies are still free to hike interest rates on future purchases, impose all kinds of fees and close accounts or lower credit limits without warning. The restrictions apply only to consumer cards, not business cards.

Consumer groups are pushing for more regulation to address those issues. They'd like the federal government to create a powerful pro-

A young woman appears shocked by the fees on her credit card statement. A January 2010 survey by the National Small Business Association showed that rates and terms on credit cards had worsened in the previous five years.

consumer regulator. The U.S. House in December [2009] passed a bill that calls for such an agency, and the [Barack] Obama administration supports it, but its future is uncertain in the Senate. Banks and business groups oppose the legislation.

Nessa Feddis, vice president and senior counsel of the American Bankers Association, says further restricting the flexibility of card issuers will hurt consumers because banks will simply refuse to offer them cards.

"Government price controls don't work, and they end up harming the people they're intended to help," she says.

Here's a summary of the major areas left untouched by the new law:

Raising and Adding Fees

Although the new law restricts certain fees, such as those charged for surpassing credit limits or paying late, plenty of other charges remain fair game. Consumer groups say card fees are like playing Whac-a-Mole: As you squash some, others pop up.

In recent months, banks have ramped up additional fees. Last year, Fifth Third Bank began charging some cardholders $19 for not using their cards for 12 months. In December, Alliance Data Systems, which issues private label cards for retailers, said it would start charging customers $1 per month to receive statements by mail. Citi has begun to charge higher rates on some cardholders who don't charge more than a certain amount.

Other banks are eyeing higher charges for annual fees, buying in foreign currencies, taking cash advances and requesting higher credit limits. Those are all permitted under the new law, though there are some new, mild restrictions on upfront fees charged during the first year of subprime accounts.

"Credit card issuers are mostly free to do whatever they want in terms of fees," says Josh Frank, senior researcher with the Center for Responsible Lending.

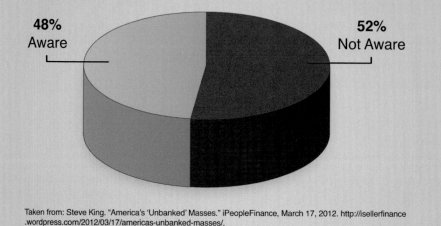

Percentage of People Aware of How the Credit CARD Act of 2009 Will Impact Them

48%
Aware

52%
Not Aware

Taken from: Steve King. "America's 'Unbanked' Masses." iPeopleFinance, March 17, 2012. http://isellerfinance .wordpress.com/2012/03/17/americas-unbanked-masses/.

Hiking Interest Rates

Although the new law heavily restricts rate hikes on existing balances, it does not prohibit card issuers from raising rates on future purchases. There's no limit to how high annual percentage rates (APRs) can go. However, after Feb. 22, banks must give 45 days notice of higher rates, and they're restricted from raising rates on accounts less than a year old.

In October [2009], a South Dakota subprime credit card marketer, First Premier Bank, raised eyebrows when it offered a card with an interest rate of 79.9 percent. Such a rate is not illegal and will not be under the new law.

"People need to watch out for the fact that there's no cap there," Bowne says.

Closing Accounts, Lowering Limits

Banks remain free to close accounts or lower credit limits without notice and for any reason. As the economy has stalled, banks are reducing their exposure, and nothing in the new law prohibits them from doing so.

Domenick Mirando, who helps run his father's towing and auto repair business in Milldale, Connecticut, was frustrated to learn there's little he can do about the issuers of his four cards chopping his available credit by about $25,000 over the past three months—money he needs for the business. After calling the offices of his attorney general and his senator, he's now consulting with bankruptcy lawyers.

"I don't know what anybody can do," says Mirando, 58, who adds that he never paid late. "It's not that it's illegal. It may be immoral, though."

Aside from being an inconvenience, the practice can also lower consumers' credit scores, which are based in part on the ratio of debt to available credit. In February 2010, a CreditCards.com national survey showed 48 percent of all cardholders reported their issuer had made a unilateral change in the past 12 months. The most-common change: 38 percent said they'd seen an interest rate increase. Another 14 percent said their credit limits were cut. A drop in consumers' credit limits can drop credit scores, which could hinder other kinds of borrowing.

Exempting Business Cards

The provisions of the law apply only to consumer credit cards—not business credit cards or charge cards. Small businesses, which have increasingly turned to credit cards as a source of financing in the economic downturn because bank loans have dried up, do not receive the law's protection if they have business or corporate accounts.

A survey released in January 2010 by the National Small Business Association showed that 68 percent of responding members said that rates and terms on credit cards had worsened in the past five years. One-quarter said they pay 20 percent interest or more on their cards.

However, the law requires the Federal Reserve to study small businesses' use of credit cards and how those companies are protected from unfair practices—an indication that Congress might consider extending some provisions to business credit cards in the future.

EVALUATING THE AUTHOR'S ARGUMENTS:

Given the limitations of the Credit CARD Act of 2009 as reported by Tony Mecia, do you agree with Jennifer Liberto in the previous viewpoint that it has been a positive change? Why or why not?

Viewpoint

3

The Government Should Place Restrictions on Payday Loans

Ray Fisman

"A clearer explanation of how costly it will be to carry the loan might save some folks from falling into the payday debt trap."

Ray Fisman is the Lambert Family Professor of Social Enterprise and the director of the Social Enterprise Program at the Columbia University Business School. In the following viewpoint he argues that payday loans should be regulated by the government. Payday loans are short-term advances with high interest rates given to consumers on the basis of the amount of their next paycheck. He reviews the findings of a study by economists from the University of Chicago who found that informing borrowers of the costly terms of the loans can deter them from taking out the loan. Fisman states that the government must intervene in some way to protect consumers from these predatory lenders.

AS YOU READ, CONSIDER THE FOLLOWING QUESTIONS:

1. According to the author, what percentage is the annual interest rate on an average payday loan?
2. How much money does the average payday loan customer borrow, according to Fisman?
3. As stated by the author, what is the average annual percentage rate for most credit cards?

There's been a lot of finger-pointing lately about who is to blame for the untenable financial circumstances of many American families. Among the usual suspects—Wall Street quants [quantitative analysts], fly-by-night mortgage brokers, the households themselves—none is an easier target than payday lenders. These storefront loan sharks are portrayed by their detractors as swindlers preying on the desperation and ignorance of the poor. A payday backlash is already well underway—Ohio recently passed legislation capping interest rates at 28 percent per year, and the Military Personnel Act limits interest charged to military personnel and their families to 36 percent. The average payday loan has an annual interest rate of more than 400 percent.

Payday lenders themselves argue that they're being victimized for providing a critical social service, helping the hard-up put food on the table and cover the rent until their next paychecks. Charging what seem like usurious interest rates, they claim, is the only way to cover the cost of making $100 loans to high-risk borrowers.

Informing Borrowers

If payday lenders really do provide a much-needed financial resource, why deprive Ohioans and American servicemen of this service? A recent study by University of Chicago economists Marianne Bertrand and Adaire Morse suggests there might be a middle ground—by allowing payday lenders to continue making loans but requiring them to better explain their long-term financial cost. In a nationwide experiment, Bertrand and Morse found that providing a clear and tangible description of a loan's cost reduced the number of applicants choosing to take payday loans by as much as 10 percent. Better information, it turns out, may dissuade borrowers vulnerable to the lure of quick cash while maintaining the option of immediate financing for those truly in need.

An average visitor to a payday loan shop expects to get a loan of around $350. Lenders typically charge a loan fee of $15 for each $100 borrowed, with the principal and interest fee to be repaid at the date of the borrower's next payday. Since most employees are paid twice a month, a customer who takes out a $100 loan each pay cycle and repays it the following one will have spent nearly $400 over the course of a year, making the annual percentage rate [APR] on the loan 400

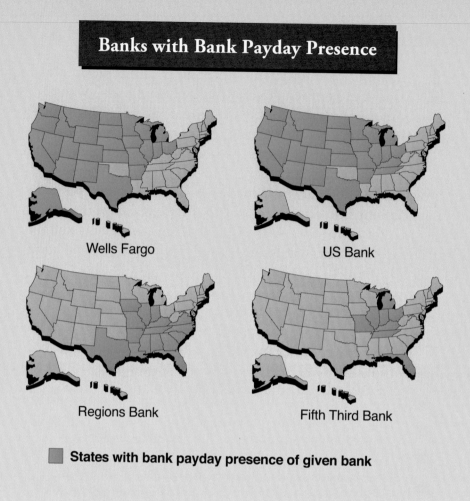

Wells Fargo

US Bank

Regions Bank

Fifth Third Bank

States with bank payday presence of given bank

Taken from: Sam Glover. "Big Banks Jump on Payday Loan Train." *Caveat Emptor*, February 16, 2012. http://caveat emptorblog.com/big-banks-jump-on-the-payday-loan-train/.

percent. (By comparison, the APR on most credit card debt is 16 percent; for a subprime loan [a loan offered to individuals who do not have good credit or who have a weak credit history], it's 10 percent.)

Before receiving the loan, borrowers sign an agreement that includes a government-mandated disclosure of this stratospheric APR. So it's natural to wonder why Bertrand and Morse would expect any further information on loan costs to have an impact on the decision of whether or not to take the loan.

The researchers argue that many payday loan customers may not know what an APR is, let alone have any basis for judging whether 400 percent is high or low. (Some states require that applicants sign a waiver confirming that they understand the APR, but they're certainly not tested for APR comprehension.) So Bertrand and Morse devised three alternative ways of explaining the high cost to borrowers and collaborated with a national chain of payday loan stores to see what effect this additional information might have on prospective payday customers in 77 stores nationwide.

On randomly selected days, in addition to receiving the usual loan paperwork, borrowers were given the option of participating in a University of Chicago study. (They were given a free magazine subscription for taking part.) The willing participants filled out a short survey on education background, level of self-control ("Do you describe yourself as a planner? Impulsive?"), purpose of the loan, and the number of weeks they expected to need to repay it. Then, instead of getting a standard-issue package with only with the loan due date printed on the front, participants received an envelope with additional information on the cost of the loan.

One group of loan applicants was presented with a table of APRs, listing the cost of payday debt relative to credit cards and subprime mortgages and highlighting the relatively high cost of payday loans relative to these other forms of financing.

The second group of prospective borrowers in the study received a chart showing the cost of using a $300 payday loan for three months ($270 in interest payments) as compared with credit card debt ($15). Here, Bertrand and Morse tested the thesis that borrowers may view each small loan in isolation, without considering the full toll that payday borrowing takes on their finances. It's $15 here . . . $15 there . . . peanuts in the grand scheme of things (hence the aptly named peanuts effect in behavioral economics). But over a few months, this adds up to real money.

Finally, the economists wanted to assess whether payday borrowers are as hopelessly optimistic about their future finances as the rest of us. Bertrand and Morse presumed that when most prospective borrowers take out a two-week loan, they expect it to be a one-time thing—only to find themselves in the same desperate situation two weeks later. To counteract this misperception, Bertrand and Morse gave a third group a chart showing the average number of times payday loans get refinanced (four out of 10 borrowers refinance at least five times).

Compared with a control group of participants who simply filled out the survey (but never got any extra payday loan info), Bertrand and Morse found that presenting borrowers with a comparison of a payday APR with the APRs on mortgages or credit cards had no effect on borrowing in the months that followed, possibly because these other forms of financing are generally unavailable to payday borrowers anyway and thus not relevant to their decisions. But the borrowers who were given a chart explaining the three-month cost of carrying a payday loan were 10 percent less likely to take a loan during subsequent months. Among those who did take additional loans, the total amount borrowed averaged around $195, as compared with $235 for the control group. The chart showing average borrower refinancing rates had little impact on the fraction of customers taking additional loans but did reduce the amount of future loans among those who continued to borrow. (Unsurprisingly, the effect of better information was greatest for those that rated themselves as cautious planners rather than impulsive spendthrifts.)

Alternative Solutions

So presenting borrowers with a clearer explanation of how costly it will be to carry the loan might save some folks from falling into the payday debt trap. But what about the other 90 percent of borrowers, who even when presented with evidence of the long-term costs still took the loan? For many of these borrowers, no amount of information will deter them. These may be candidates for what [social scientists] Richard Thaler and Cass Sunstein call a "nudge" out of payday borrowing. Economists Dean Karlan and Jonathan Zinman have proposed just such a nudge: mandating a cooling-off period before a payday loan clears to discourage impulsive borrowers (though this runs somewhat counter to the purpose of a payday loan, which is for people who need money *now*).

A recent policy paper by Michael Barr (now assistant secretary of the treasury for financial institutions [until 2010]), co-authored with behavioral economists Sendhil Mullainathan and Eldar Shafir, puts the payday lending business in the context of the larger problem of a banking sector that doesn't address the needs of the poor and unbanked. Among their suggestions is a tax credit for banks that provide safe and affordable accounts and lending services for the poor.

All of these ideas recognize that we don't live in a world of perfectly informed consumers making rational decisions in well-functioning markets. This research and these proposals come at a time when the

Payday loan services argue that their high interest rates are the only way to cover the cost of making loans to high-risk borrowers.

myth of the rational market has exploded. The White House, meanwhile, is now occupied by an administration that may be willing to use the hand of government—guided by the work of researchers like Bertrand and Morse—to give payday borrowers the information they need to make decisions that serve their own interests rather than those of the finance industry.

EVALUATING THE AUTHOR'S ARGUMENTS:

On the basis of the data Ray Fisman provides, should the government regulate payday loans? If so, in what ways? If not, why not?

Restricting Payday Loans Can Hurt Consumers

"Banning payday lending in these uncertain times would drive consumers further down the 'lending ladder.'"

Todd Zywicki and Astrid Arca

Todd Zywicki is a senior scholar at the Mercatus Center, and Astrid Arca is an alumna of the Mercatus Center MA Fellowship at George Mason University. In the following viewpoint they argue that regulating payday loans will only hamper consumers in need of short-term funds. Payday loans have existed for more than a century, and borrowers are savvy enough to understand the loan terms. Furthermore, Zywicki and Arca state that restricting payday lending can lead to lenders increasing the terms of other parts of the loan, borrowers turning to other, often unsavory, lenders, and even the amount of loans made available to consumers being limited.

AS YOU READ, CONSIDER THE FOLLOWING QUESTIONS:
1. As stated by Zywicki and Arca, what percentage of the population uses payday lenders each year?
2. According to the Federal Deposit Insurance Corporation, as cited by the authors, how much interest would a customer repaying a twenty-dollar overdraft fee accrue in two weeks?
3. What is credit rationing, as explained by the authors?

Todd Zywicki and Astrid Arca, "The Case Against New Restrictions on Payday Lending," *Mercatus on Policy*, January 11, 2010. Reproduced by permission.

In the wake of the financial crisis, Congress is considering new regulations on non-traditional lending products like payday lending, although there is no evidence that such products were related in any way to the financial crisis. If enacted, the principal legislation, H.R. 1214 (the Payday Loan Reform Act of 2009), would limit the charge for a single-payment loan to an effective 391 percent annual rate ($15 per $100 two-week loan). H.R. 1214 also purports to limit borrowers to one loan at a time from a single lender, prohibit rollovers, and limit borrowers to one extended repayment plan every six months. Economic theory and empirical evidence strongly suggests that these paternalistic regulations would make consumers worse off by limiting their choices to unappealing alternatives. Also, the act would do little to protect consumers from concerns of over-indebtedness and high-cost lending. [Editor's note: H.R. 1214 was passed by the House of Representatives in 2011 but was not passed by the Senate.]

The Payday Loan Industry

Payday lending arose in big cities as early as the 1880s as an alternative to pawn shops and "chattel lenders," serving as a valuable source of short-term, small-amount lending to wage earners with steady employment but a critical need for short-term emergency funds. Since then, the payday loan industry has grown rapidly during the past two decades, from under 200 offices in the early 1990s to over 22,800 offices at the end of 2005. Forty percent of payday loan customers earn $25,000–50,000 per year, and 56 percent earn $25,000–75,000. Still, despite the intense regulatory attention on payday lending in recent years, only about 2 percent of the population (9 to 14 million people) use payday lenders in any given year. The aggregate outstanding principal balance of all payday loans at any given time is about $2 billion.

Use of payday loans is almost always precipitated by an unexpected expense that the borrower could not postpone, such as a utility bill, fear of a bounced check, healthcare expenses, or the need for funds for vacation or Christmas. In one survey of payday loan borrowers, 86 percent of respondents reported that they "strongly" (70.8 percent) or "somewhat" agreed (15.7 percent) that their use of a payday lender was to cope with an unexpected expense.

Lack of access to emergency funds can be detrimental to consumers. For instance, every bounced check can incur substantial fees and impose indirect costs. If a check is [for] an insurance payment, the policy will be terminated; if it's for utilities, such as telephone or electricity, it may lead to termination of service, penalties, and a substantial security deposit to reconnect service. Bouncing a check may also result in termination of a bank account and even a risk of criminal prosecution, while also damaging the individual's credit score, making subsequent access to credit even more difficult.

Payday loan customers are not fools; they have carefully weighed all of their options and chosen the best alternative they can afford. Payday lending customers choose this financing option over an array of relatively unattractive options, such as pawn shops, bank overdraft protection, credit card cash advances (where available), and informal lenders or loan sharks. For instance, according to a study by the Federal Deposit Insurance Corporation, a customer repaying a $20 debit overdraft in two weeks would incur an average Annual Percentage R[ate] (APR) of 3,520 percent, which can be an unattractive alternative for a borrower.

FAST FACT

According to Colleen Creamer of the *Nashville Ledger,* the payday loan industry takes in $42 billion a year.

Payday loan customers are also well informed about the cost of these loans. According to [economist Gregory] Elliehausen, only 2 percent of payday loan customers reported that they did not know the finance charge for their most recent new payday loan; 94.5 percent reported finance charges consistent with prevailing market prices. . . .

Since their inception, regulators have expressed concern about the apparent high cost of short-term, small loans. However, and in light of the recent economic turmoil, anecdotal reports indicate that as a result of a reduction of access to credit, and especially a dramatic reduction in the availability of credit-card credit, middle-class consumers and small businesses increasingly are turning to non-traditional lenders, such as payday loans and pawn shops. Banning payday lending in these uncertain times would drive consumers further down the "lending ladder" to pawn shops or alternatives that are not economically desirable.

The Economics of Usury Regulation

Misguided paternalistic regulation that deprives consumers of access to payday loans is likely to force many of them to turn to even more expensive lenders or to do without emergency funds. This is because substantive regulation, such as price caps on interest rates (often referred to as "usury" regulations), limits the interest rate of loans made to borrowers. This can have several unintended consequences that can be extremely harmful to consumer welfare, which can be summarized under three basic headings: term re-pricing, product substitution, and credit rationing.

Term re-pricing describes the process by which lenders offset limits on what they can charge on regulated terms. By increasing the price of other terms of the loan or related loan products, like the minimum required amount of the loan, lenders can amortize the costs of issuing the loan over a higher loan amount. As reported by Policis [social and economic research group], this can force borrowers to borrow larger amounts than they prefer or can reasonably manage, thereby reducing the usefulness of the loan and, perversely, promoting over-indebtedness.

The second unintended consequence of usury regulation, product substitution, arises when certain types of regulation make it impossible to price a particular consumer loan product in a manner that makes it economically feasible for the lender and borrower to enter into a transaction, leading lenders and borrowers to search for alternative, less-desired credit products. For instance, a recent study of U.S. consumers found that in states with strict usury ceilings, unbanked consumers tended to substitute pawn shops while those with access to mainstream credit markets made greater use of retail and revolving credit.

Pawn shop loans are especially unappealing: Their cost is comparable to payday loans, but they require the borrower to part with personal property to use as collateral. In addition, because of the small size ($76 on average) and high transaction cost of pawn shop loans, these are of limited usefulness in managing financial difficulties. Moreover, those forced to substitute greater use of revolving credit likely end up paying even higher costs for credit and run into greater financial difficulty. Both credit card delinquencies and delinquency-related revenues are higher in states with interest-rate ceilings that squeeze payday lending out of the market.

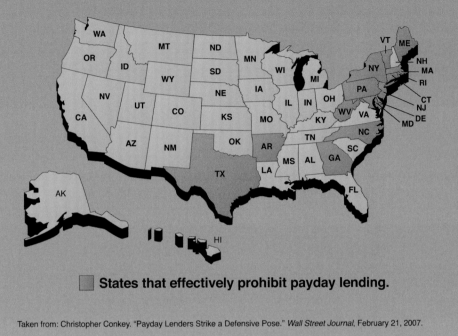

States That Effectively Prohibit Payday Lending

States that effectively prohibit payday lending.

Taken from: Christopher Conkey. "Payday Lenders Strike a Defensive Pose." *Wall Street Journal*, February 21, 2007.

Finally, regulation may result in rationing of credit to particular borrowers if it is impossible for them to obtain any formal credit on affordable terms. Such rationing could force borrowers to turn to the informal sector (friends and family or illegal loan sharks) or to do without credit. In 2006, Japan severely tightened its rate ceiling on consumer loans (as in the United States; many consumer loans were also small-business loans), resulting in a two-thirds drop in consumer loan acceptances in the two years following the enactment of the law. During that period, Japan saw a dramatic growth in illegal loan sharking, primarily run by organized crime (Yamiken lenders). Japanese consumers who admit to having contacted a loan shark during a 12-month period were twice as numerous among those who were unable to borrow as much as they wanted from a legitimate consumer finance lender (26 percent) as among those who were able to obtain the amount that they wanted (13 percent). Those declined by legitimate lenders were also more likely to contact loan sharks (27 percent) and even more likely among those who had been asked to provide guarantors or collateral for a loan (42 percent). As might be expected, illegal lending costs much more than legitimate lending, and collections by illegal lenders rest on threats, intimidation, violence, and forms of exploitation.

People Need Credit

Essentially, foreclosing viable options for credit because they are thought to be too expensive does not make the need for credit go away—if a low-income person needs $500 for a car repair in order to get to work, eliminating payday lending as an option does not eliminate the need for the car repair. It simply forces the borrower to find funds elsewhere or live without the car, which could adversely affect job performance.

Economists have almost uniformly concluded that usury regulations that force these changes in lending and borrowing behavior is harmful to consumer welfare. Regulations that encourage substitution from one type of high-cost credit to another or encourage a more confusing and opaque price scheme are unlikely to make consumers better off. Once lenders make adjustments and offsetting behaviors in response to substantive regulations, the benefits to be gained from interest-rate caps are clearly understood as small and the costs from the unintended consequences as extremely large. Consumers are left with fewer choices, higher borrowing costs, and less flexibility.

EVALUATING THE AUTHOR'S ARGUMENTS:

Ray Fisman in the previous viewpoint argues for regulation of payday lending, while this viewpoint's authors, Todd Zywicki and Astrid Arca, argue that regulation will only hurt poor consumers. Are consumers hurt more by payday lending practices or regulations to those practices? Cite from the viewpoints in your explanation of your position.

Chapter 3

Who Should Be Responsible for Paying Off Debt?

The National Debt Clock in New York City keeps track of America's debt. The figure shown was the debt on January 22, 2011. As of February 5, 2013, it was 16,505,657,300,000 and increasing by over 2 million dollars per minute.

The US Government Must Raise the Debt Ceiling

"Raising the debt limit ... [is] just a matter of paying bills that we've already incurred."

William Gale

William Gale is a senior fellow at the Brookings Institution and codirector of the Urban-Brookings Tax Policy Center. In the following viewpoint he argues in favor of raising the nation's debt ceiling, or debt limit. He states that by raising the ceiling, the US government would simply be paying off debts it already owes. He notes that raising the debt ceiling has been done many times in the nation's history and that it is unrelated to managing other financial problems. In fact, not raising the debt ceiling and defaulting on debts will likely harm the future fiscal strength of the nation. Gale is certain that the debt ceiling will be raised; it is just a matter of time.

AS YOU READ, CONSIDER THE FOLLOWING QUESTIONS:

1. As described by Gale, what is the debt limit?
2. How many times has the debt limit been raised in the last fifty years, as stated by the author?
3. If the debt limit is not raised, how much does Gale say Congress will have to cut annually in federal taxes to pay the nation's debts?

T he debt limit is the maximum amount of debt the federal government can legally issue at a point in time. The current limit will be reached in the next few months [midyear 2011], prompting discussion over whether Congress should raise the limit. As with so many deliberations in Washington, though, the popular discussion on this topic is shrouded in confusion and ignorance, and masks the real issues.

The underlying issue is simple: If you spend your income on things you want, and the charges then show up the following month on your credit card bill, would you pay those charges? Yes, of course you would. You've made purchases and the bill has come due.

That's the whole question about raising the debt limit—whether Congress should allow the government to pay for spending that has already been approved by Congress. (Remember, it is Congress that authorizes all federal spending.) The answer, of course, is yes.

Congress's Joint Select Committee on Deficit Reduction was a bipartisan compromise on the debt-ceiling crisis.

The Issue at Hand

Now, as you're paying your credit card bill, you may well conclude that you are spending too much or that you need to earn more income to pay for your current standard of living. But that would be a separate issue, and stiffing the people who supplied the goods you just bought not only wouldn't resolve that problem, it would in fact make solving it harder, because your credit rating might fall if you don't pay what you already owe.

Likewise, the separate problem for the U.S. government is how to deal with our dismal fiscal future. The nation needs to resolve the looming fiscal imbalance through spending cuts and tax increases. Not paying the bills we already owe—that is, not raising the debt limit—not only won't solve the real problem, it would actually make a solution more difficult by undercutting the government's credit-worthiness.

In short, raising the debt limit has nothing to do with controlling future spending or with raising the taxes necessary to pay for future spending. It is just a matter of paying bills that we've already incurred.

Raising the debt limit is a completely ordinary event. The limit has been raised 74 times in the last 50 years and 10 times in the last 10. Debt limit increases are associated with both Republicans and Democrats. When federal debt approaches the limit, the president typically favors raising the limit and the other political party demagogues the move. That is exactly what is happening right now.

Talk of refusing to raise the debt limit is just that—talk. Not raising the limit would require Congress to annually find about $1.3 trillion in federal tax increases or spending cuts—a set of policy changes larger than the revenues currently raised by the individual income tax. So far, the legislators who say they oppose a debt limit increase have not come forth with anything near such a plan. Nor should you expect them to. They are just blowing smoke. Eventually, they will agree to raise the limit.

FAST FACT

As of September 2012, the US debt ceiling was set at $16.394 trillion, according to the US Treasury Department.

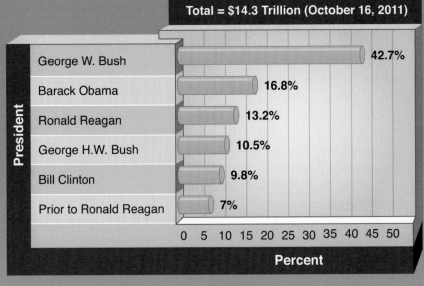

Percentage of National Debt Incurred by US Presidents

Total = $14.3 Trillion (October 16, 2011)

President	Percent
George W. Bush	42.7%
Barack Obama	16.8%
Ronald Reagan	13.2%
George H.W. Bush	10.5%
Bill Clinton	9.8%
Prior to Ronald Reagan	7%

Taken from: Barry Ritholtz. "US Debt Accumulation by President." The Big Picture, October 16, 2011. www.ritholtz.com/blog/2011/10/us-debt-accumulation-by=president/.

While voters and members of Congress may find it cathartic to channel their outrage and frustration at the underlying budget situation onto the current debt limit discussion, the real question is how to adjust future spending and taxes to bring about future fiscal stability and sanity. The sooner we get to that discussion, the better.

Refusing to raise the debt limit not only would not help solve that problem, it would actually make a solution much harder to achieve.

EVALUATING THE AUTHOR'S ARGUMENTS:

After reading the viewpoint, do you agree with William Gale? Should the debt limit be raised? What pieces of evidence swayed your opinion one way or the other?

Viewpoint

2

The US Government Should Not Raise the Debt Ceiling

Deroy Murdock

"Congress should not hike the debt limit, period."

In the following viewpoint Deroy Murdock, a nationally syndicated columnist with the Scripps Howard News Service, argues that the debt ceiling should not be raised. Instead, he says, Congress should work on paying down existing debt. Murdock states that the issue is further complicated by myths being spread about taxes paid by wealthy Americans. Wealthy Americans do pay hefty taxes, he notes, and turning the nation against them will only hurt workers in the corporate-aircraft and yacht-building industries. Instead, he asserts, Congress should make use of unused funds in program accounts and tax profits of foreign subsidiaries of US corporations.

Deroy Murdock, "Don't Raise the Debt Ceiling," *National Review,* July 14, 2011. Copyright © 2011 by National Review. All Rights Reserved. Reproduced by permission.

AS YOU READ, CONSIDER THE FOLLOWING QUESTIONS:

1. According to the April 2009 Congressional Budget Office report, as cited by Murdock, how much did the top 1 percent of taxpayers pay in 2006?
2. By what percentage did American yacht sales decline following former president George H.W. Bush's luxury tax on yachts, according to the author?
3. What percentage does the US government own of Arizona and Nevada, according to Murdock?

Team [Barack] Obama's debt-limit negotiating position is fueled by a central non sequitur, a core myth, and a spectacular oversight. Correcting these deficiencies would help Democrats and Republicans drain America's Olympic pool of red ink without drowning the economy in tax hikes.

Respecting the Debt Cap

First, the idea that the federal debt ceiling must be raised in order to lower federal indebtedness is the logical equivalent of a high-speed train derailment. Responsible consumers awash in debt do not beg credit-card companies to hike their borrowing limits. Instead, they freeze their credit thresholds and pay their debts, ideally until their finances are back in the black.

Obama's insistence on raising the debt limit is like saying, "You are right, MasterCard. I am tapped. So, I will forgo theater tickets and skip my annual ski trip. Now, please raise my limit by $5,000." MasterCard's customer-service representative would explode into laughter.

Congress should not hike the debt limit, period. The staggering sum of $14.3 trillion should remain the Everest [i.e., the peak] of U.S. financial irresponsibility from which Uncle Sam must descend. This will be arduous but far healthier than climbing into ever-more-vertiginous [dizzying] debt and triggering an all-consuming avalanche of unpayable bills.

Furthermore, the notion that leaving the debt limit intact will trigger default is another monstrous lie designed to bamboozle the

American public and cow Republicans into retreat. As with a credit card, default means neglecting one's bills rather than respecting a debt cap. If Visa refuses to augment a customer's credit line, default occurs only if he stops making minimum payments. Indeed, as his balance drops, his credit rating improves.

America must do this.

The Myth of Wealthy Taxpayers

For Fiscal Year 2011, Treasury expects $2.23 trillion in revenues, from which it must pay bond holders $213 billion in interest. As Sen. Pat Toomey (R., Pa.) explains, if Treasury can manage this, America will not default.

Meanwhile, Democrats pollute the proceedings with the core myth that the wealthy do not pay their fair share of taxes. These marina-dwelling slackers, their argument goes, devour caviar while the American worker toils to keep Washington operating. This narrative capsizes reality, and leading Democrats know it. Yet they bellow otherwise:

"Pay up," Sen. Frank Lautenberg (D., N.J.) demanded last week [in July 2011]. "Don't let the fat cats sit there purring nicely while they watch events unfold."

Senate Democratic leader Harry Reid of Nevada sponsored a resolution on "the Sense of the Senate on Shared Sacrifice." It demanded that Americans who earn more than $1 million annually "make a more meaningful contribution to the deficit-reduction effort."

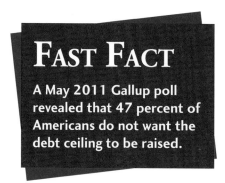

FAST FACT

A May 2011 Gallup poll revealed that 47 percent of Americans do not want the debt ceiling to be raised.

Lautenberg and Reid are savvy enough to recognize their own words as demagoguery.

According to an April 2009 Congressional Budget Office [CBO] report, in 2006 (the most recent data available) the top 1 percent of taxpayers made at least $332,300 annually and paid 28.3 percent of *all* federal taxes. The top 10 percent (earning $98,100 or more) paid 55.4 percent of all federal taxes. Meanwhile, the bottom

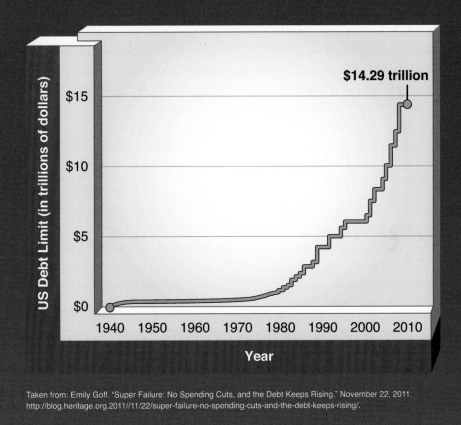

Increases to the US Debt Limit, 1940–2010

$14.29 trillion

US Debt Limit (in trillions of dollars)

$15

$10

$5

$0

1940 1950 1960 1970 1980 1990 2000 2010

Year

60 percent of taxpayers earned up to $47,399. They paid 14 percent of all federal taxes.

Regarding effective federal tax rates, CBO reported April 4 that in 2007, all taxpayers averaged a 20.4 percent tax rate. However, the top 1 percent effectively paid 29.5 percent, and the top 10 percent paid 26.7 percent. The bottom 20 percent of taxpayers paid an effective rate of just 4 percent.

So, the notion that the evil rich are paying less than their "fair share" is yet another lie that infects this debate. If it is insufficient that the top 10 percent pay 70 cents of each federal tax dollar, what would suffice—80 cents? 95? 100?

Attacks on Corporate-Jet Owners

Obama's contribution to this deceit is an obsession with company aircraft.

"The debt ceiling should not be something that is used as a gun against the heads of the American people to extract tax breaks for corporate-jet owners," Obama said July 6, [2011,] deploying both class-warfare rhetoric and firearms imagery that Democrats denounced after Jared Lee Loughner's alleged shootings of Rep. Gabrielle Giffords (D., Ariz.) and 19 others in Tucson last January.

Obama's comments might hold a droplet of water if the wealthy assembled their own jets in their driveways, from Bel Air [California] to Palm Beach [Florida]. Instead, approximately 120,000 largely unionized employees at general-aviation manufacturing companies produce these planes. As the "Jobs President" browbeats this sector, he further jeopardizes those positions.

"We are perplexed over recent comments and actions questioning the value of corporate aircraft," International Association of Machinists [IAM] president R. Thomas Buffenbarger and General Aviation Manufacturers Association CEO Peter J. Bunce wrote President Obama in a June 29 labor-management letter. "During the severe economic downturn in 2008, ill-informed criticism of corporate jets and business aviation exacerbated the challenges facing our industry," they added. "More than 20,000 highly skilled IAM members were laid off. . . . We are very concerned that the rhetoric coming from some in your Administration will lead to similar economic difficulties."

Obama repeatedly has attacked the accelerated-depreciation treatment given to corporate aircraft—never mind that it was part of his vaunted $814 billion "stimulus." Rather than use his very own legislation as a Weapon of Class Destruction, Obama should aid the entire economy by expanding this narrow provision so that all businesses may write off purchases immediately—whether for executive jets or for shovels.

Instead, Obama fires at the rich in the air, while Reid torpedoes them in the water. He told colleagues on July 6, "Millionaires, billionaires, oil companies, and the owners of yachts and jets don't need special tax breaks the rest of Americans don't get."

Does Reid really want to sail into that tempest again?

When Americans read Daddy Bush's [former president George H.W. Bush] lips in October 1990, he imposed a 10 percent "luxury tax" on $100,000-plus yachts, perhaps to prove that he could lash fellow plutocrats [wealthy rulers]. Instead, he and Congress (including Reid) clobbered blue-collar yacht builders. As the Cato Institute's Michael Tanner recalls, billionaires bought their boats in Barbados, Bush's get-tough tax sank American yacht sales by 70 percent, and U.S. vessel makers scuttled 25,000 employees. In 1993, after the tax generated little revenue amid the shipwreck it created, Congress overwhelmingly killed it.

Reid now aches to make that mistake again.

Unused Funds

Finally, a spectacular oversight plagues Democrats and Republicans alike. As Sen. Tom Coburn (R. Okla.) and Rep. David Schweikert (R. Ariz.) observe, some $703 billion in forgotten funds languish in untouched accounts across the federal budget. When Congress authorizes, say, $1 billion for a program, an unspent $250 million, for instance, just sits there. These coins between the cushions of the

President Barack Obama addresses the press about the debt-ceiling crisis in July 2011. The nation's debt has become a political football with a lot of grandstanding by both parties.

national sofa exceed TARP's [the corporate bailout program] original $700 billion budget! Schweikert's Forgotten Funds Act would apply this dusty money to debt reduction. Why on Earth is this massive sum not on the table?

Washington can generate revenues for immediate debt reduction without increasing taxes:

Some $1 trillion in profits languish among the foreign subsidiaries of U.S. corporations. Repatriating this potential growth capital, perhaps at a temporary, 10 percent Welcome Home tax rate (versus America's sky-high 35 percent corporate tax) would pump $100 billion into debt elimination and $900 billion into private-sector innovation and job creation.

Washington owns 48 percent of Arizona and 84.5 percent of Nevada. What if it sold a quarter of this property? Selling parcels of the federal estate would generate revenue and decrease the cost of mismanaging far more land than Washington can handle. Should visitors expect a geo-thermal power plant 100 feet from Yellowstone's Old Faithful geyser, as [environmental group] Greenpeace predictably will huff and puff?

No.

While developing natural resources on some non-sensitive lands makes sense, why not let governors convert some federal property into state parks? Why not sell some federal acreage for vacation cabins or fly-fishing retreats—neither of which involves oil derricks?

Wouldn't it be nice if Democrats abandoned their galactic deception and hateful class-warfare? What a wonderful world it would be if Republicans were less timid about proposing deep budget cuts, agency closures, and revenues that did not impose tax hikes on this wheezing economy. Imagine what an attractive debt-reduction deal America might enjoy if Democrats were honest and Republicans were courageous.

EVALUATING THE AUTHOR'S ARGUMENTS:

After reading William Gale's and Deroy Murdock's viewpoints, who do you think presents better evidence for raising or lowering the debt ceiling? Explain.

Parents Should Be Cautious in Paying Off Their Children's Debts

"When parents think about whether to bail out a child from debt, more than money is at stake."

Sarah Angle

In the following viewpoint Sarah Angle, a writer for Fox News and Mannatech, Inc., argues that parents should be careful about bailing their adult children out of debt. She states that parents should consider the long-term effects of their bailout. It may simply make their children more financially dependent. She recommends that parents make their children fill out loan papers and pay interest on any money given. In addition, she warns that bailing adult children out of debt can strain family relations. She further cautions that bailouts should not be given if they impair the parents' retirement plans.

AS YOU READ, CONSIDER THE FOLLOWING QUESTIONS:
1. According to the author, what is the first question parents should ask themselves before bailing their child out of debt?
2. What four steps does Angle outline for determining whether an adult child qualifies for a loan?
3. How can parents find the Applicable Federal Rate for charging interest on the loan they give to their child, according to the author?

When Jeff and Patricia Banks paid off their son's $6,000 credit card debt, they thought they were doing him a favor. Their 24-year-old son Eric was paying the card's minimum balance each month at a hefty 22 percent interest rate. So, instead of paying a credit card company, he would pay back Mom and Dad, save himself a huge chunk of change in interest, and become a financially smart, stable adult.

That was the theory. Unfortunately, when it comes to family and finance, things don't always work out as planned. When parents think about whether to bail out a child from debt, more than money is at stake. Says psychotherapist and co-author of "The Financially Intelligent Parent," Dr. Eileen Gallo. "It's never a cut and dried answer . . . you have to look at the situation."

Helping Versus Hurting

Gallo says that when deciding whether to bail a child out of debt, the first question parents should ask themselves is: "Will this action foster my child's independence or extend their dependence?"

As a parent, your goal is to provide your children with the skills they need to grow into successful, responsible, happy adults, right? So, Gallo asks, what is your action teaching your child? "If parents continually rescue their kids, they are helping them stay dependent." If you're going to help, Gallo says, make sure it's real help—which means evaluating the child's financial history and asking why they're in debt to start with. When you can answer the "why?" question, you'll begin to understand where this behavior is coming from and if paying off the debt is really in the child's best interest.

Do They Qualify for a Loan?

There are many emotions involved when it comes to family and finances, says Charles Schwab financial consultant Richard Rosso, so it helps to look at the loan from a more analytical perspective. Rosso recommends taking these steps before signing over a check:

Step 1: Evaluate the child's past financial history. Was the child responsible with money growing up? Was he or she a saver or a spender?

Step 2: Write down a list of questions you want to ask the child. Think about the type of questions a lender asks before awarding a loan, such as job history, additional outstanding debts, collateral and savings.

Step 3: Write down the child's answers to your questions and use those answers to help formulate your lending decision.

Step 4: Have the child make a detailed budget (or give you a copy of one if it already exists).

Before giving a teen a credit card, parents should evaluate their child's financial history, ask questions of the teen that a lender would ask, evaluate their answers, and have the teen make out a detailed budget.

Sign on the Dotted Line, Junior

Now that you've got something to work with (other than pure parental emotion!) you're ready to make an educated decision.

At this point, if your head and heart are screaming, "Yes, I do want to help my baby out of debt!" just remember the devil is in the details. Before you even think about writing a check, set up a clear—no questions asked—set of guidelines to ensure that you and your child know what's what.

North Carolina financial consultant Beth Gregg suggests signing a parent-child contract. The contract should list clear payment due dates and monthly payments. It should also address the consequences of not paying or paying late.

What about interest? If you do decide to charge it, Gregg says, have it written into the agreement. To avoid having the IRS [Internal Revenue Service] consider the loan as a gift, charge, at a minimum, what the IRS calls the Applicable Federal Rate. To find that rate, go

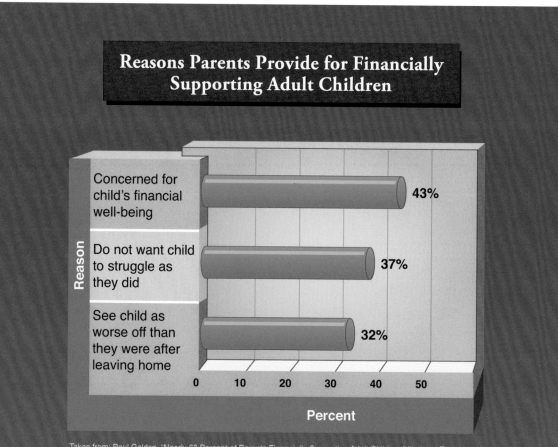

Taken from: Paul Golden. "Nearly 60 Percent of Parents Financially Supporting Adult Children." National Endowment for Financial Education, May 26, 2011.

to the IRS website, search for "applicable federal rate" and click on the first link. Table 1 contains the loan rate you need—select the one that matches the length of your loan.

Family + Money = Messy

Asked later if he was glad his parents paid off his credit card debt, Eric hesitates. "It was good, in a way," he says. "At the time it seemed like a good deal. But now, thinking back, it wasn't such a good choice."

Owing his parents money makes things awkward, says Eric. "The only time I really feel comfortable hanging out with them is at the first of the month—when we've paid off everything and we're caught up. If it's at the end of the month, Dad always brings up money."

"You can ruin a family over money," says Gregg. "Because it's never just a business decision, and a lot of times not everything works out as planned."

Case in point: Eric. Besides straining family relationships, he's still overspending, not saving and relying on the generosity of his parents to make his life work. To add

> **FAST FACT**
>
> A 2011 survey conducted by the National Endowment for Financial Education (NEFE) reveals that 59 percent of parents are financially supporting or have supported their adult children after their children finished college.

fuel to the fire, Eric's wife has chosen not to work. So Jeff and Patricia don't feel like the couple is doing all they can to repay the debt. The family's problem: There were no initial guidelines set up between Eric and his parents. So now there are no clear expectations or rules to follow.

We know this type of financial situation can affect the relationship between parent and child, but according to Rosso, it can affect the dynamics of the entire family. "When a parent loans money to a financially irresponsible child, it can create animosity between other children in the family," explains Rosso. "Siblings who aren't getting a bailout may feel that Mom and Dad are being taken advantage of. They empathize with the parents and have animosity toward the brother or sister getting the loan."

Keep an Eye on Your Retirement

Most parents have an innate tendency to put their children first, and finances are no exception. As sweet and selfless as that may be, it can come back to hurt you and your retirement.

"Parents need a real black-and-white picture of how much money they need to live on before offering to pay off a child's debt," says Gregg. "You sacrifice so much for your kids and then say, 'My gosh, I can't do what I want to do after working for 40 years.'"

Jeff Banks says the $6,000 they used to pay off Eric's credit card didn't really hurt them financially. And looking back, he says he would still do it again. "But I would hope for a better outcome . . . that Eric would have stayed in the clear and not messed up his credit. But in the overall perspective of giving things to your kids, $6,000 isn't a big deal."

EVALUATING THE AUTHOR'S ARGUMENTS:

After reviewing the evidence provided by the author, Sarah Angle, do you think that parents should help their children out of debt? Explain your answer.

Son, Can You Spare a Signature? Kids Co-Sign for Credit Strapped Parents

Lyneka Little

"A child lending to a parent is almost reversing the relationship and could cause problems."

Lyneka Little covers personal finance and other money-related issues for a variety of publications, including the *Wall Street Journal* and *O, the Oprah Magazine.* In the following viewpoint Little states that as the nation's economic problems intensify, more people will find themselves in difficult financial situations. Little argues that adult children should avoid helping their parents out of debt. Not only does it strain familial relations, but it could harm the adult child's credit should the parent default on the debt. In addition, she says, relying on adult children for financial help is difficult for parents, who have traditionally been the caretakers in the relationship.

"Son, can you co-sign for my car?" That's the kind of question more adult children like Daniel Lee have heard from parents hit hard by the great recession.

"[My father was] working in the diamond industry when the housing boom happened; he started investing in housing and, unfortunately, when the housing market went down, he started losing money," leaving his credit damaged, Lee, a Miami-based computer programmer, says.

Lee's retired father, 65, began having difficulty keeping up with his mortgage payments as the housing market soured, and late mortgage and auto payments began to tarnish his credit. His father's newly checkered credit made it difficult to maintain a car and that's when his son stepped in.

After the credit crunch, record unemployment levels and financial Armageddon, many parents have chucked the norm and sought credit help from their children, financial planners say.

Evidence of such an increasingly popular arrangement has popped up in a few places. Although the number of parents co-signing for adult children has risen to 11 percent from 9 percent in the past two years, the number adult children helping parents with a car lease has increased more than 30 percent, according to LeaseTrader.com, an online car-leasing website.

The adult children, defined as people ages 20 to 29, have been assisting parents who are 40 to 55.

The business of co-signing is a tricky proposition for adult children, especially those struggling to pay back their college loans or looking to save for a house.

"I got so much from him, I don't think that the short-term, 15-month lease, and the total amount for the lease, is going to destroy my life," Lee, 29, says.

The nation's economic woes appear to be adding to the burden. Fifty-six percent of bankruptcy debtors last year were ages 35 to 54, according to the Institute for Financial Literacy (http://www.financial lit.org/resources/2009Demographics.htm#Age). While the number of debtors between the ages 18 and 44 shrank, the number of bankrupt debtors ages 45 and up climbed slightly from 2008.

Foreclosures, unemployment and the overall health of consumer credit may be "forcing adults to make this decision and take this alternative approach," says John Sternal, vice president of marketing communications at Miami-based LeaseTrader.com.

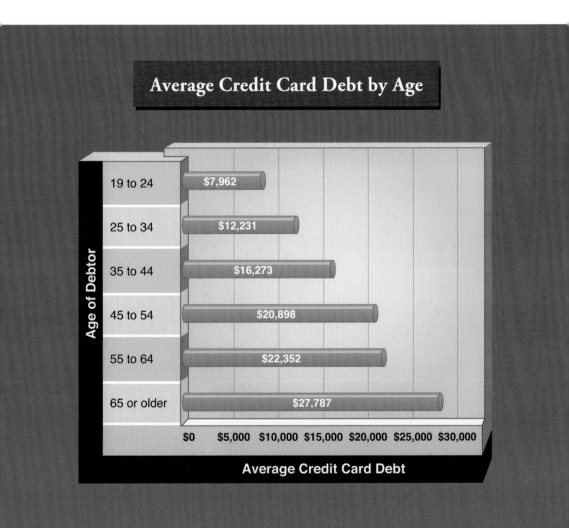

Average Credit Card Debt by Age

Measuring the Risk of Helping Parents

But the financial alternative comes with pitfalls when a co-signer becomes liable for the full loan if a parent fails to pay. "One of the problems of co-signing is you usually don't know there's a problem until the loan is in default," says Rick Kahler, a financial planner at Kahler Financial Group in Rapid City, S.D.

"If a payment is missed, you're one of the last to find out."

A collection agency will go after a co-signer as aggressively as the original debtor. And, unfortunately, unlike a bank, a co-signer cannot repossess an auto loan if parents fall behind on a financial obligation.

Also, "late payment can blow someone's credit score by 100 points," says Sergei Lemberg, an attorney at consumer law firm Lemberg & Associates LLC in Stamford, Conn. "A single missed payment can cost you thousands of dollars."

A parent's failure to make timely payments could also result in higher interest for credit cards and other lines of a credit, and could affect mortgage approval rates.

What's more, co-signing on a loan turns a familial relationship into a business one. "You have to be ready to pay off that loan," Kahler says.

Children should avoid helping their parents get out of debt because it could strain family relations and affect the children's credit should the parents default on their loans.

"If you think it's a wise thing to do, then, of course, go for it but you still must say, 'I'm going to be just fine if I have to step in and make this good because that's the bottom line.' The bottom line is you've got to be ready to pay off that note."

For Lee, there was no hesitation. "When I needed him, he was there for me," Lee says, adding that he pays the majority of the $280 car lease.

The Good, the Bad, and the Ugly

Of his decision to co-sign rather than buying his father the car, Lee says, "it's going to help him begin to rebuild his credit."

"I didn't want everything in my name. He's on the lease because I wanted his name on the registration, and I wanted him to be part of it because it's his car," Lee adds.

But not all families handle the arrangements so effortlessly.

"I need opinions please; I feel forced to co-sign on a mortgage for my parents . . . ," a Twitter user wrote a week ago, sharing in anonymity the qualms many children face when asked to co-sign.

From another user: " . . . More important things to worry on. Dad wants me to co-sign on a car."

And it's no cake walk for the parents, either.

> **FAST FACT**
>
> Thirty states have filial responsibility laws, which require children to pay for their parents' debts, including nursing home bills, according to the National Center for Policy Analysis.

"A parent having to swallow very hard and ask their adult child to co-sign for a car loan means the parent is in financial distress and not able to obtain the loan though their own credit worthiness," says Gail Cunningham, vice president of public relations for the National Foundation for Credit Counseling, a financial education and counseling service based in Silver Spring, Md.

The parent-child relationship generally "has the parent being in charge and child being obedient," says Theodore Connolly, author of personal finance book "Road Out of Debt."

Co-signing, he says, unwittingly creates a master-servant situation, and the person that owes the money falls into a different status. "A child lending to a parent is almost reversing the relationship and could cause problems," he adds.

A few experts were split about how to seal the deal, but most agree that parent and child should be prepared to pay if there are any hic-cups during repayment of a loan.

That's why Lee and his father picked a Toyota RAV4 compact when deciding on a new vehicle.

"Of course, I'm not going to take a lease for a brand new Mercedes," Lee says. "I'm not going to take a lease that's going to destroy my life."

But any child who resists should consider offering alternatives to avoid souring the parental relationship, some experts say.

Declining to co-sign can be "explosive when you include the family dynamics of the situation because we're not logical with these deci-sions," South Dakota financial planner Kahler says.

Remember that you're in an adult role, not a child's. And instead of simply declining, explain the downside and ask if there are other ways to help.

Given that his own father almost went bankrupt after co-signing on an employee's business loan, Kahler suggested offering to give the item to the parent as a gift, or putting the loan in the child's name to give complete control of the assets.

While there may be no way to avoid upsetting your parents, there are valid reasons to decline, credit counselor Cunningham says.

"If your mom, dad or parents have demonstrated financial irre-sponsibility their whole life and you feel you're enabling them by co-signing, speak the truth in love," she says. "Or, if opening a new line of credit could impact your credit score."

Lee's solution was to minimize the impact.

"We looked at a short-term lease and not something like 36 months," he says, "so I made my risk much smaller."

EVALUATING THE AUTHOR'S ARGUMENTS:

After reviewing the evidence provided by author Lyneka Little, do you think adult children should help their par-ents get out of debt? Why or why not?

Facts About Debt

Editor's note: These facts can be used in reports to add credibility when making important points or claims.

Facts About Young People and Debt

According to Jumpstart Coalition for Personal Financial Literacy:
- One out of three high school seniors uses credit cards;
- 50 percent of all high school seniors who use credit cards have ones issued in their names.

According to the Federal Reserve Bank of Boston:
- The average age at which a US consumer under the age of 35 first adopts a credit card is 20.8 years; the average age of credit card adoption for a consumer over the age of 65 is 40.6 years.

According to the FINRA Investor Education Foundation:
- In 2009, 41 percent of cardholders from the ages of eighteen to twenty-nine made only the minimum required payment on a credit card in some of the past twelve months.

According to Javelin:
- Just 51 percent of Americans aged eighteen to twenty-four indicated they had used a credit card in the month preceding the September 2008 survey; 71 percent of that age group said that they had used a debit card in the same period.

According to the 2006 Charles Schwab Foundation's "Teens and Money Survey":
- While the majority of surveyed teens say they are knowledgeable about how to write a check (61 percent) and use a debit card (54 percent), fewer than half (41 percent) know how to balance a checkbook;
- the majority of teens say they know how to shop for the best deal when making a purchase (66 percent), but fewer than half understand how to budget their money (48 percent);
- nearly 31 percent of teens surveyed owe money to either a person or a company;

- on average, teens owe $230, with older teens aged sixteen to eighteen owing significantly more than younger teens aged thirteen to fifteen ($351 vs. $84);
- 14 percent of teens aged thirteen to eighteen say they already are more than a thousand dollars in the red, and this percentage rises significantly for teens sixteen to eighteen (22 percent);
- nearly half (46 percent) of all teens who owe money admit being concerned about paying it back;
- 34 percent of survey respondents say they get money from a debit or credit card—either in their own or their parent's name;
- 18 percent of teens say that if given the choice they would rather make purchases with a credit card than with cash.

Facts About College Costs and Debt

According to Demos.org:
- 13 percent of households whose current credit card balance includes some college expenses report leaving school to deal with credit card debt;
- 18 percent of households identify late payments toward student loans as contributing to their low credit score;
- graduating college seniors leave school with an average of over twenty-five thousand dollars in student loan debt.

According to Project Student Debt:
- 33 percent of bachelor's degree recipients graduate with private loans, with an average private loan amount of $12,550;
- the unemployment rate for young college graduates rose from 8.7 percent in 2009 to 9.1 percent in 2010, the highest annual rate on record;
- the unemployment rate for twenty- to twenty-four-year-olds with only a high school education was 20.4 percent in 2010.
- the median income for those with only a high school diploma or its equivalent in 2010 was $26,349, more than 40 percent less than the median income for college graduates.

According to the Council of Independent Colleges:
- Student loan debt is now nearing $1 trillion, and the delinquency rate for student loans has increased to 8.9 percent;
- one-third of students who graduate with a bachelor's degree do not have any educational debt;

- students enrolled at independent colleges are twice as likely to receive grants from their institutions as students enrolled at public institutions, and they are more than three times as likely to receive grants as students at for-profit institutions.

Facts About Low- and Middle-Income Households Carrying Credit Card Debt

According to Demos.org:

- 40 percent of households used credit cards to pay for basic living expenses such as rent or mortgage bills, groceries, utilities, or insurance in the past year because they did not have enough money in their checking or savings accounts, a rate comparable to 2008;
- nearly half of households carried debt from out-of-pocket medical expenses on their credit cards. The average amount of medical credit card debt was $1,678;
- 86 percent of households who incurred expenses due to unemployment in the past year took on credit card debt as a result;
- while 62 percent of overall indebted households reported that their credit was "excellent" or "good," only 44 percent of African Americans and 55 percent of Latinos described their credit in such positive terms.

Facts About Small Businesses and Debt

According to the National Small Business Association:

- Credit cards are now the most common source of financing for America's small-business owners;
- 44 percent of small-business owners identified credit cards as a source of financing that their company had used in the previous twelve months—more than any other source of financing, including business earnings; in 1993, only 16 percent of small-business owners identified credit cards as a source of funding they had used in the preceding twelve months.

According to the May 2010 *Report to the Congress on the Use of Credit Cards by Small Businesses and the Credit Card Market for Small Businesses*:

- As of the end of 2009, 83 percent of small businesses used credit cards, 64 percent used small-business cards, and 41 percent used personal cards;

- an estimated 64 percent of small firms (with fifty or fewer employees) used business credit cards either for borrowing or transacting business in 2009;
- more than 20 percent of firms applying for credit cards were not able to get a card, and another 5.6 percent did not accept the card because of unfavorable terms.

Facts About the National Debt

According to the US Treasury Department:
- The total public outstanding debt on October 11, 2012, was $16,157,753,419,211.

According to CNN Money:
- In 2009, 11.3 million, or nearly 25 percent, of all mortgage borrowers owe more on their loans than their homes are worth.

According to the Employee Benefit Research Institute's 2012 Retirement Confidence Survey:
- Americans' confidence in their ability to retire comfortably is stagnant at historically low levels—just 14 percent are very confident they will have enough money to live comfortably in retirement (statistically equivalent to the low of 13 percent measured in 2011 and 2009);
- many workers report they have virtually no savings and investments—in total, 60 percent of workers report that the total value of their household's savings and investments, excluding the value of their primary home and any defined benefit plans, is less than twenty-five thousand dollars.

Facts About Worldwide Debt

According to the World Bank:
- In 2006 the debts of the developing world totaled $2.7 trillion;
- for every $1 in aid a developing country receives, over $25 is spent on debt repayment.

According to economist Lydia Fisher of the *Huffington Post*:
- The current world debt is $160 trillion (governments, corporations, individuals), of which some $40 trillion is world government debt, of which $14.3 trillion is US government debt.

Organizations to Contact

The editors have compiled the following list of organizations concerned with the issues debated in this book. The descriptions are derived from materials provided by the organizations. All have publications or information available for interested readers. The list was compiled on the date of publication of the present volume; the information provided here may change. Be aware that many organizations take several weeks or longer to respond to inquiries, so allow as much time as possible for the receipt of requested materials.

American Bankruptcy Institute (ABI)
44 Canal Center Plaza, Ste. 400, Alexandria, VA 22314
(703) 739-0800
e-mail: support@abiworld.org
website: www.abiworld.org

ABI is a multidisciplinary, nonpartisan organization committed to advancing research and education on matters related to insolvency. Its professional membership comprises attorneys, accountants, auctioneers, judges, lenders, academics, turnaround specialists, credit professionals, and many others. ABI offers access to its consumer bankruptcy resources for a fee in an online database titled the Consumer Bankruptcy Center. The organization also publishes the *ABI Journal,* the *ABI Law Review,* newsletters, and cases studies.

American Enterprise Institute (AEI)
1150 Seventeenth St. NW, Washington, DC 20036
(202) 862-5800
fax: (202) 862-7177
website: www.aei.org

AEI is a private, nonpartisan, not-for-profit institution dedicated to research and education on issues of government, politics, economics, and social welfare. The AEI's program on financial services covers accounting; banking; insurance, securities, and futures regulation;

corporate governance; and consumer finance. The AEI's financial services publications include "Unfree to Choose: The Administration's Consumer Financial Protection Agency," "Regulation Without Reason: The Group of Thirty Report," and "What Should Society Want from Corporate Governance?"

Americans for Fairness in Lending (AFFIL)
7 Winthrop Square, 4th Fl., Boston, MA 02110
(617) 841-8000
e-mail: info@affil.org
website: www.affil.org

AFFIL is dedicated to reforming the lending industry in order to protect Americans' financial assets. AFFIL works to educate and advocate for American consumers and small businesses. In addition to a regularly updated blog, AFFIL's website offers opinion statements about lending practices, including "Credit Card Law's Effect on People Under 21" and "A New Era for Credit Cards."

Center for American Progress (CAP)
1333 H St. NW, 10th Fl., Washington, DC 20005
(202) 682-1611
fax: (202) 682-1867
e-mail: progress@americanprogress.org
website: www.americanprogress.org

CAP is a think tank dedicated to improving the lives of Americans through ideas and action. CAP combines policy ideas with a modern communications platform to help shape the US national debate, challenge conservative philosophy, and urge the media to cover issues that truly matter to most Americans. In a core focus area that addresses the economy, CAP concentrates on such topics as markets and regulation, credit and debt, the global economy, housing, and more. Publications that concern economic issues include "Putting Credit Card Debt on Notice," "Card Sharks," and "What Bank Mergers Mean for Credit Cards."

Center for Responsible Lending (CRL)
302 W. Main St., Durham, NC 27701
(919) 313-8500
website: www.responsiblelending.org

CRL is a nonprofit, nonpartisan research and policy organization dedicated to protecting homeownership and family wealth by working to eliminate abusive financial practices. CRL has conducted or commissioned landmark studies on predatory lending practices and the impact of state laws that protect borrowers. It also publishes many resources for consumers, including fact sheets on payday loans, overdraft loans, and mortgages.

Consumer Action (CA)
221 Main St., Ste. 480, San Francisco, CA 94105
(415) 777-9635
fax: (415) 777-5267
website: www.consumer-action.org

CA is a nonprofit membership-based organization that was founded in San Francisco in 1971. During its more than three decades, Consumer Action has continued to serve consumers nationwide by advancing consumer rights and publishing educational materials in multiple languages, including Managing Money, a financial literacy clearinghouse. Among its many publications, several focus on debt, such as "Debt Consolidation: Is It for You?" and "Families and Credit Cards."

Consumer Federation of America (CFA)
1620 Eye St. NW, Ste. 200, Washington, DC 20006
(202) 387-6121
e-mail: cfa@consumerfed.org
website: www.consumerfed.org

Since 1968, the CFA's professional staff has gathered facts, analyzed issues, and disseminated information to the public, policy makers, and the rest of the consumer movement. The size and diversity of the federation's membership—approximately 280 nonprofit organizations from throughout the nation, with a combined membership exceeding 50 million people—enables CFA to speak for virtually all consumers. In addition to original studies, the CFA regularly publishes brochures and fact sheets available for free to the public, including "Building Wealth Not Debt," "Managing Your Debts," and "Your Credit Score."

Consumers Union (CU)
101 Truman Ave., Yonkers, NY 10703-1057
(914) 378-2000
website: www.consumersunion.org

CU is an independent, nonprofit organization dedicated to working for a fair, just, and safe marketplace for all consumers. The organization strives to change legislation and the marketplace to favor the consumer's interest. CU publishes the monthly periodical *Consumer Reports* and two newsletters, *Consumer Reports on Health* and *Consumer Reports Money Advisor*. The CU website also hosts a blog called *Tightwad Tod*, in which CU money reporter Tod Marks advises consumers on how to find deals and avoid scams.

Consumer Watchdog (CWD)
1750 Ocean Park Blvd., Ste. 200, Santa Monica, CA 90405
(310) 392-0522
fax: (310) 392-8874
e-mail: admin@consumerwatchdog.org
website: www.consumerwatchdog.org

CWD (formerly the Foundation for Taxpayer and Consumer Rights) is a nationally recognized consumer group that has been fighting corrupt corporations and politicians since 1985. Over the years, CWD has worked to save Americans billions of dollars by speaking out on behalf of patients, ratepayers, and policyholders. In addition to serving as a clearing of financial information, CWD publishes books regarding consumer advocacy, including *Corporateering: How Corporate Power Steals Your Personal Freedom.*

Demos
220 Fifth Ave., 5th Fl., New York, NY 10001
(212) 633-1405
fax: (212) 633-2015
e-mail: info@demos.org
website: www.demos.org

Demos is a nonpartisan public policy research and advocacy organization founded in 2000. One of the organization's core advocacy initiatives is the Economic Opportunity Program, which focuses on the economic insecurity and inequality that affects American society. The program offers analysis and policy proposals designed to provide new opportunities for young adults and financially strapped families seeking to achieve economic security. Demos publishes numerous books, reports, and briefing papers. Those that address consumer debt include "The Plastic Safety Net; How Households Are Coping in a Fragile Economy," "Borrowing to Make Ends Meet: The Rapid Growth of Credit Card Debt in America," and *Strapped: Why America's 20- and 30-Somethings Can't Get Ahead.*

Federal Deposit Insurance Corporation (FDIC)

550 Seventeenth St. NW, Washington, DC 20429
(877) ASK-FDIC (275-3342)
e-mail: publicinfo@ftc.gov
website: www.fdic.gov

The FDIC is an independent governmental agency committed to maintaining stability and public confidence in the nation's financial system by insuring deposits; examining and supervising financial institutions for safety, soundness, and consumer protection; and managing receiverships. As part of its overall mission, the FDIC supports a consumer protection initiative that provides resources to educate and protect consumers, revitalize communities, and promote compliance with government regulations and fair-lending laws. The FDIC publishes a number of alerts related to consumer spending and debt management, including "Credit Cards: New Law Protects Consumers from Surprise Fees, Rate Increases, and Other Penalties," "Managing Your Money in Good Times and Bad," and "Take Charge of Your Credit Cards."

Federal Trade Commission (FTC)

600 Pennsylvania Ave. NW, Washington, DC 20580
(877) FTC-HELP (382-4357)
website: www.ftc.gov

Established in 1914, the FTC pursues vigorous and effective law enforcement and creates practical and plain-language educational programs for consumers and businesses. The FTC also administers a wide variety of consumer protection laws, including the Telemarketing Sales Rule, the Pay-Per-Call Rule, and the Equal Credit Opportunity Act. In addition to an annual "Performance and Accountability Report," the FTC regularly publishes consumer protection materials, including "Credit and Your Consumer Rights" and "Knee Deep in Debt."

National Association of Consumer Advocates (NACA)
1730 Rhode Island Ave. NW, Ste. 710, Washington, DC 20036
(202) 452-1989
fax: (202) 452-0099
e-mail: info@naca.net
website: www.naca.net

NACA is a nationwide organization of more than fifteen hundred members who represent and have represented hundreds of thousands of consumers victimized by fraudulent, abusive, and predatory business practices. NACA's members and their clients are actively engaged in promoting a fair and open marketplace that forcefully protects the rights of consumers, particularly those of modest means. NACA's website serves as a clearinghouse of information about predatory lending practices, debt collection abuse, and credit reporting problems.

National Association of Consumer Bankruptcy Attorneys (NACBA)
2300 M St., Ste. 800, Washington, DC 20037
website: www.nacba.org

Founded in 1992, NACBA is a national organization dedicated to serving the needs of consumer bankruptcy attorneys and protecting the rights of consumer debtors in bankruptcy. NACBA comprises more than four thousand members located in all fifty states and Puerto Rico. NACBA files amicus briefs in selected appellate and Supreme Court cases that could significantly impact consumer bankruptcy rights. Many of these briefs are available on the NACBA website.

National Consumer Law Center (NCLC)
7 Winthrop Square, Boston, MA 02110-1245
(617) 542-8010
fax: (617) 542-8028
e-mail: consumerlaw@nclc.org
website: www.consumerlaw.org

NCLC is an organization dedicated to helping consumers, their advocates, and public policy makers use consumer laws on behalf of low-income and other vulnerable Americans seeking economic justice. A top priority for NCLC is providing support on issues involving consumer fraud, debt collection, consumer finance, energy assistance programs, predatory lending, and sustainable home ownership programs. NCLC publishes several items for consumers, including *Surviving Debt* and *Foreclosure Prevention Counseling: Preserving the American Dream.*

National Foundation for Credit Counseling (NFCC)
801 Roeder Rd., Ste. 900, Silver Spring, MD 20910
(800) 388-2227
website: www.nfcc.org

Founded in 1951, the NFCC promotes a public agenda for achieving and maintaining financially responsible behavior. Its member counselors are committed to delivering high-quality financial education and counseling services to millions of Americans. Its publications include *Better Fortunes: Control Your Money, Control Your Life; More than One Way Out: Personal Bankruptcy Consequences and Alternatives;* and *Live a Richer Life: A Roadmap to Personal Financial Health Following Bankruptcy.*

The Project on Student Debt
2054 University Ave., Ste. 500, Berkeley, CA 94704
(510) 559-9509
e-mail: info@projectonstudentdebt.org
website: www.projectonstudentdebt.org

The Project on Student Debt works to increase public awareness of the circumstances surrounding the need to borrow funds to pay for higher education and the implications that this necessity has on families, the economy, and society. Recognizing that loans play a critical role in making college possible, the project is committed to identifying cost-effective solutions that expand educational opportunity, protect family financial security, and advance economic competitiveness. Its publications include "Denied: Community College Students Lack Access to Affordable Loans," "Private Loans: Facts and Trends," and "Quick Facts About Student Debt."

Truth About Credit
44 Winter St., Boston, MA 02108
(617) 747-4330
website: http://truthaboutcredit.org

Truth About Credit is a project of the US Public Education Fund and the Student PIRGs (Public Interest Research Groups). Both organizations conduct research, provide education, and offer advocacy on behalf of consumers. To protect student consumers, the Truth About Credit project aims to reduce student exposure to the worst credit practices that trap them into unfair terms and conditions. Some of its most recent publications include "The Campus Credit Card Trap" and "Characteristics of Fair Campus Credit Cards."

US Department of the Treasury

1500 Pennsylvania Ave. NW, Washington, DC 20220
(202) 622-2000 · fax: (202) 622-6415
website: www.ustreas.gov

The Treasury Department is the executive agency responsible for promoting economic prosperity and ensuring the financial security of the United States. The department is responsible for a wide range of activities, such as advising the president on economic and financial issues, encouraging sustainable economic growth, and fostering improved governance in financial institutions. In addition to fact sheets and press releases, the Treasury's website includes many publications, such as "Protecting American Credit Card Holders" and "Regulations for the Credit Reporting Industry."

For Further Reading

Books

Boss, Shira. *Green with Envy: Why Keeping Up with the Joneses Is Keeping Us in Debt.* New York: Warner, 2006. The author argues that trying to compete materially with each other is keeping Americans in debt and unhappy.

Butler, Tamsen. *The Complete Guide to Personal Finance: For Teenagers and College Students.* Ocala, FL: Atlantic, 2010. A guide created to teach teenagers about many financial matters, it includes how to save money, how to create a checking account, and how to obtain and use credit cards.

Dijkstra, A. Geske. *The Impact of International Debt Relief.* New York: Routledge, 2008. The author examines the effects of international debt forgiveness in eight Latin American and African nations.

Draut, Tamara. *Strapped: Why America's 20- and 30-Somethings Can't Get Ahead.* New York: Doubleday, 2006. The author addresses the challenges facing young Americans as they enter the financial marketplace and provides solutions for ensuring a successful economic future.

Fisher, Sarah Young, and Susan Shelly. *The Complete Idiot's Guide to Personal Finance in Your 20s and 30s.* Indianapolis: Alpha, 2009. A simply written financial primer for young people just beginning their adult lives.

Hansen, Mark Victor. *The Richest Kids in America: How They Earn It, How They Spend It, How You Can Too.* Miami: Hansen House, 2009. This book focuses on child entrepenuers and their spending and investment strategies.

Levine, Judith. *Not Buying It: My Year Without Shopping.* New York: Free Press, 2006. In an effort to break their overspending habits, the author and her partner spend a year attempting to make no new purchases beyond necessities.

Mundis, Jerrold J. *How to Get Out of Debt, Stay Out of Debt, and Live Prosperously.* New York: Bantam, 2012. The author offers solutions for consumers of all incomes to get out of debt once and for all.

Nagler, JoAnneh. *The Debt-Free Spending Plan: An Amazingly Simple Way to Take Control of Your Finances Once and for All.* New York: American Management Association, 2013. Suggestions for developing a way to live on a cash-only basis are provided.

Schor, Juliet B. *Born to Buy: The Commercialized Child and New Consumer Culture.* New York: Scribner, 2005. The author argues that children are being targeted by companies in ways they have never been before, which is greatly contributing to a culture that is focused on consumption and the accumulation of debt.

Scurlock, James D. *Maxed Out: Hard Times in the Age of Easy Credit.* London: HarperCollins, 2007. The author argues that the credit industry exploits impoverished Americans to increase profit margins.

Periodicals

Anderson, Jessica L., and Kimberly Lankford. "Live Debt-Free," *Kiplinger's Personal Finance,* November 2008.

Badenhausen, Kurt. "Debt Weight Scorecard," *Forbes,* February 8, 2010.

Businessweek. "Degrees of Debt," September 10, 2012.

Cheney, Karen. "Don't Let Debt Weigh You Down," *Money,* May 2012.

Clark, Jane Bennett. "The Dark Side of Student Debt," *Kiplinger's Personal Finance,* June 2011.

Coy, Peter. "Debt: The Forgiveness Fix," *Businessweek,* August 11, 2011.

Dell, Kristina. "I Owe U," *Time,* October 31, 2011.

Esswein, Patricia Mertz, and Kimberly Lankford. "Escape the Debt Trap," *Kiplinger's Personal Finance,* February 2012.

Fisher, Daniel. "The Global Debt Bomb," *Forbes,* February 8, 2010.

Frick, Robert. "Why Debt Won't Die," *Kiplinger's Personal Finance,* April 2012.

Gordon, John Steele. "A Short History of Debt," *American History,* October 2011.

Greider, William. "Debt Jubilee, American Style," *Nation,* November 14, 2012.

Jefferson, Aisha. "Debt-Free Diet," *Black Enterprise,* January 2012.

Judis, John B. "Doom!," *New Republic,* October 6, 2011.

Karabell, Zachary. "Debt Doesn't Matter," *Time,* November 8, 2010.

Kiplinger's Personal Finance. "The Lure of Student Loan Forgiveness," November 2012.

Kristof, Kathy. "Crushed by College," *Forbes,* February 2, 2009.

Lorin, Janet. "Debt for Life," *Businessweek,* September 10, 2012.

Mallaby, Sebastian. "You Are What You Owe," *Time,* May 9, 2011.

Malpass, David. "The U.S. Needs a New Debt Limit," *Forbes,* February 27, 2012.

Moran, Gwen. "Digital Debt Relief," *Entrepreneur,* April 2012.

Morgan, Richard. "Liberating Education," *Fast Company,* September 2012.

Nation. "End Student Debt," May 21, 2012.

Poppick, Susie. "Just the Facts About the Deficit," *Money,* May 2012.

Reason. "Cut the Debt by Cutting Government," August/September 2011.

Resnick, Rosalind. "A Debt-Free Philosophy," *Entrepreneur,* October 2010.

Scaliger, Charles. "Paying Down U.S. Debt Before It's Too Late," *New American,* April 9, 2012.

Silver-Greenberg, Jessica, and Peter Carbonara. "Public Debts, Hired Guns," *Businessweek,* March 23, 2009.

Smith, LaToya. "Debt Snowball Method," *Black Enterprise,* June 2012.

Tennant, Michael. "Hitting the Ceiling or Going Through the Roof?," *New American,* June 6, 2011.

Wild, Russell. "No Shortcuts to Debt Relief," *Saturday Evening Post,* January/February 2012.

Williams, Jeffrey. "Academic Freedom and Indentured Students," *Academe,* January/February 2012.

Zakaria, Fareed. "The Debt Deal's Failure," *Time,* August 15, 2011.

Index

Picture Credits